THE BUMPY ROAD

A Memoir of a Journey from Shanghai

Abby L. Jiang

For Wei Tong Liu, 刘伟通, my one of a kind uncle.

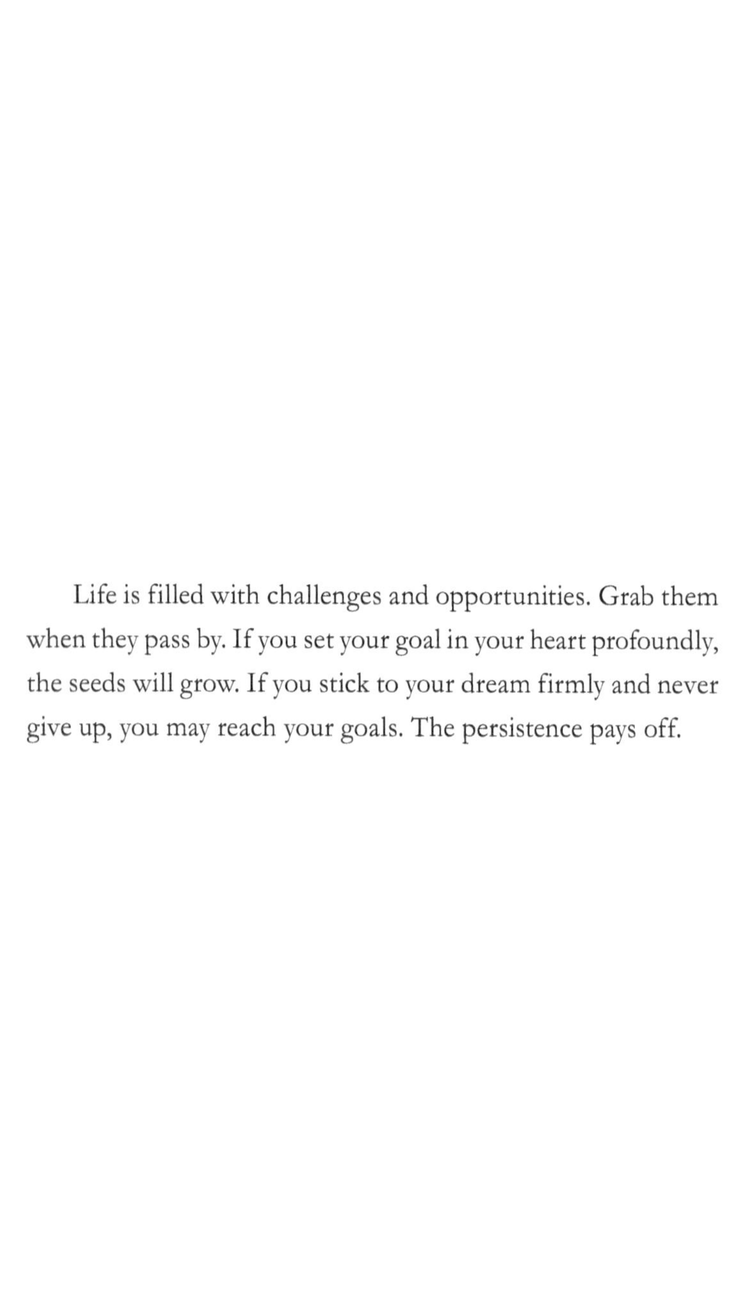

Life is filled with challenges and opportunities. Grab them when they pass by. If you set your goal in your heart profoundly, the seeds will grow. If you stick to your dream firmly and never give up, you may reach your goals. The persistence pays off.

CONTENTS

PREFACE

Once in a while, a colleague would ask what college I attended. While seemingly a simple question with a simple answer, my path to formal education was disrupted by the Chinese Cultural Revolution when I was twelve years old. Schools were closed by the government, many of my plans for the future were suddenly thwarted, and I never quite recovered. So, to answer a colleague's question about college is to call up some of the most devasting moments of my life and the history of modern China, making it difficult to put my story into words even today. However, after listening to the experiences from my journey to college in the U.S., I'm often told, "You have to write about this. Oh my God, I had no idea of such history!"

Taking their advice, this is my story.

Growing up, I watched China struggle to find its position in the modern world as I struggled to find my own identity. After I finished my last day of fifth grade, the Cultural Revolution started and China went mad in every way possible. All schools were closed for almost two years. Education was always important in my family. I was a model student, but overnight, I went from top of my class to "bad blood" when the Cultural Revolution singled out my family for political persecution.

My parents were denounced by the Red Guards as capitalists simply because my father had inherited my grandfather's business. Nobody dared to show their anger towards the Communist government. Many innocent people were beaten to death or committed suicide, their fates unknown to loved ones.

The Cultural Revolution pulled me from the comforts of upper-class life to an average working-class existence. My family never fully recovered from being put into the "Bad #6" category.

The school closure during the Cultural Revolution in the summer of 1966 was a life-changing event for many Chinese youths. When the secondary schools reopened after a year and a half, I was surprised to see the new textbooks were thinner than they had been before: anything the Revolution opposed had been edited out. The high school curriculum was also reduced from six years to four years. During those four years, students were mandated to serve several months out in the countryside and factories for "re-education."

Nobody ever evaluated these students' education levels after the schools reopened. We were called four-year secondary school graduates. The colleges were closed for about eleven years, so the oldest and youngest students in my college class could be as far as fifteen years apart, with very different levels of educational attainment.

I was one of the very lucky few who passed the national college exam, which led to an enormous change in my personal life for the better. My college education allowed me to see the world from different angles, and I finally moved to the U.S. in 1987.

However, when I reflect on my life, I often regret not having a solid secondary school education. My regular education stopped at the fifth grade. That was a crime that the Cultural Revolution inflicted on a whole generation of kids. I would never want my children to miss what I missed in my youth.

I brought my daughter, Crystal, to New Jersey when she was seven. The June 4 Tiananmen Square incident in 1989 shocked me to my core. I immediately moved Crystal from Shanghai to the U.S.

With a Chinese-American daughter in the house, I learned more about cultural differences than ever before.

From my daughter's fine education in the U.S., I saw what a different world we now lived in. I realized that the Western ideologies my uncle taught me were growing from the soil here. Or, I should say, it was rooted in the European/American culture. I immediately felt at home in this world that was at once so new and so familiar.

This is not only the story of my life during the Cultural Revolution; it is also the story of an immigrant mother and how she raised her daughter, who went on to become a Princeton graduate, in unfamiliar territory. Immigration to the U.S. is not an easy experience. It requires great courage. But if it makes the first generation after me stronger and changes the next generation's life thereafter, it will be worth all the struggle.

Looking around, when I meet some Chinese friend who was born here and has become a successful professional, I often ask myself: if I had grown up in a different place, would I be another person? I hope you will be able to find the answer after reading this memoir.

PART I

ONE HOT SUMMER NIGHT

It was a sultry summer evening. The sky shone blue with a light haze, typical for June in Shanghai. Families gathered in the *long-tang* as the sun sank slowly behind the endless red roofs of the tenements.

Behind wide boulevards, a maze of winding lanes and alleys were interconnected, serving as the social connection to the beating heart of the city. People were gossiping, playing cards, or just people-watching. The streets were humming with the sounds of birds and cicadas, laughter, and chatter. Kids were running around while the adults waited for the cool breezes.

The air soon hung heavy with the sweet, tangy soy smells of roasted scallion noodles. It was almost dinner time. The whole neighborhood was out. The weather-beaten wooden doors were flung open. I was curled up in a bamboo recliner, reading a book outside the old door of our stone gate home, a curved vine of wisteria hanging high from the tall wall weeping with the wind.

Shanghai, which means City on the Sea, lies on the Yangtze River. The summer winds blew past the old black wooden door, bringing on cool evening pleasure. It was my favorite spot in which to read. My grandmother, having just taken her shower, sat next to me with a palm leaf fan in hand. My father was listening to his usual classical music, and my mother was doing her routine cleaning after dinner.

Suddenly, a strong wind came from nowhere. I looked up at the sky: it was turning dark, and rain was approaching. I got up, took my book, and was ready to move inside.

Then I heard *pa-pa-pa*, fast footsteps approaching from behind. Turning around, I was stunned to see about a dozen young men and women rushing to our front door. Calling my father's name loudly, and ignored my grandmother and ran inside our house. They immediately occupied our living room. I saw my father quickly turn off his record, then put on a set of formal clothes over his shirt before talking to them. I was too far away to hear what they were saying. My father's face held a mix of worry, surprise, and confusion. I ran upstairs to my bedroom and shut the door behind me. I was scared but had no clue what would happen next.

Ten minutes later, a small crowd of neighbors gathered in the middle of the *long-tang*, near the entrance to our house. A young man, who appeared to be the group leader, held a loudspeaker in one hand and read quotations from the copy of Chairman Mao Zedong's *Little Red Book* he clutched in his other hand. No one paid any attention to him but waited to see what would come next.

Mao's book was the only material allowed to be read, like a special bible in Red China during the Proletarian Cultural

Revolution.[1] Often, reading Mao's quotations was an opening for a rally. More people came out of their homes to watch.

Later I learned that those people who came to my house were from my father's company and were part of the so-called "Red Guard." The Red Guard movement mobilized in 1966. They raided private homes and confiscated or demolished property defined as part of old bourgeois culture.

They destroyed homes, burning books and smashing possessions, especially priceless antiques. They detained, interrogated, and even beat their targets. Mao expressed his support and approval of the Red Guard movement, saying, "It's right to rebel."

The Red Guards came into our house without a search warrant or any other legal authority. This sounds crazy today, but it was a normal, everyday occurrence in China in the latter half of 1966, at the beginning of the Cultural Revolution. In our neighborhood, a few families had been raided before us by the Red Guards. Most of them were wealthy businessmen, academics, or intellectuals who'd never done anything against the law. The Red Guards invaded without warning. Some of their victims could not tolerate the denouncement and humiliation. They took their own lives not long afterwards. There were too many precious lives lost and too many happy families ruined.

---

1   The Cultural Revolution was launched in China in 1966 by Communist leader Mao Zedong in order to reassert his authority over the Chinese government. Believing that Communist leaders were taking the Party, and China itself, in the wrong direction, Mao called on the nation's youth to purge the "impure" elements of Chinese society and revive the revolutionary spirit that had led to victory in the civil war twenty years earlier and the formation of the People's Republic of China. The Cultural Revolution continued in various phases until Mao died in 1976, and its tormented and violent legacy would resonate in Chinese politics and society for decades to come.

I was twelve years old then. That night, I was curious, and a bit frightened. What were the intruders doing? Why did they yell at my father? With questions storming through my head, I was called to go outside by the Red Guards.

It was humid and warm after a summer rain. The air was still. About forty people stood outside, many of them were good neighbors and my playmates. I saw my father and mother standing in the center, with their heads lowered. They looked nervous but calm and did not say anything to me. I saw their worries toward me. We had not spoken to each other since the intruders came.

The leader was a young man standing in the center of the crowd. He was agitated and yelled at the top of his lungs, saying that my father was a capitalist, so he was a bad person, and much more besides… Nobody in the audience said anything. When the rally finished, the crowd dispersed, and everyone went home.

My parents looked very tired. Dad walked with me back home, whispering in my ear, "I am sorry, baby. Your father did something wrong." He looked confused and scared. I did not say anything.

These Red Guards posted several large pieces of white paper on our front door. They had written in black ink brush pen with large-sized characters that my father was a bloodsucker and a capitalist. I hated it whenever I saw it, but I was not allowed to remove them. I knew my father was innocent.

As the oldest son, Dad inherited my grandfather's eyeglass company. That was his only sin. He got a label: capitalist. During the peak madness of the Cultural Revolution, even if you were innocent, the safest thing to do was obey and agree with anything the Communists said. Even when they cooperated, though, some people still got ill-treated or beaten to death. With the support of Chairman Mao, the Red Guards moved with full power and speed to "destroy the old society and build a new one," as a typical slogan said. My next-door neighbor had been the victim of a similar raid a few days earlier. He was an entrepreneur and owned a furniture factory. My dad had talked about it that dinner time in a sad mood. Now I understood why.

That night, I was too nervous and exhausted to sleep, waiting for my mom to come to my bedroom, but she never showed up. I left my small bronze fan on and eventually fell asleep without knowing what time it was.

When I woke up the next morning, my parents were still downstairs, and the Red Guards were there whole night too! They had dug out our courtyard flowerbeds looking for gold, I was told, searching tirelessly for the family money.

I looked around my home: all the drawers were open; papers and clothes were over the floors… I was shocked! I bit my tongue, but it hurt. I was not in a dream.

My uncle Wei Tong and his wife Jinhua Li lived on the third floor. The Red Guards left them alone because he had not joined my grandfather's business. For now, they let him off the hook.

While I was having breakfast the following day, Auntie Jinhua came to me. "Would you like to go with me to my school during the day?" she asked.

"Yes, of course. I'd love to!" I answered. Auntie taught English in high school. There were always so many interesting things going on in her workplace. I loved to explore, but she rarely let me and was always busy with her students. Now I was thrilled. Putting on my backpack quickly, I headed out with her during the rush hour.

Later in her school, I overheard her say to a colleague, "The child did not do anything wrong. The environment at home is not good for kids." She was trying to protect me.

Anywhere was better than being home. It was summer vacation, so the school had no students, but some teachers still came to work. Compared to home with the cold Red Guards, everyone in Auntie's school was so warm.

I enjoyed my week there so much. Every day, I wandered around the campus and did my summer vacation homework while listening to the birds singing on the tree branches.

In China, students had homework assignments every day when schools closed for the summer. The Chinese educators believed that the learning process should be continuous.

Auntie did not have children. From that day on, everyone in her school learned that she had a niece who was like her own daughter. I became well-known there overnight.

I did not have any inkling as to what would follow, but that hot summer night was carved in my memory forever. It hurts to remember it even after so many years. My simple but happy childhood was suddenly interrupted and turned upside down. The world never was the same again.

CHAPTER 2

ADOPTION

Two days later, I was in the kitchen when a Red Guard woman called on me. My parents were not home, so she told me a story I never knew.

She took me outside my house, where no one was around, and said with a mysterious look, "Do you know that you are adopted?"

"What do you mean?" I looked at her with disbelief. "No, I do not." But I did not dare to question how she'd learned this news.

"You are not blood-related to this family. So you do not have to protect them. You should stand with us and tell me all you know, like where your father hid his gold." They had been searching in vain overnight.

I never knew if we had gold in the house and, of course, I never saw any. What could I say? I looked into her eyes, seeing a wolf under sheepskin smiling back at me.

When I told her I knew nothing, she was clearly disappointed. After a few minutes of thinking, she let me go. I felt so relieved.

However, I never had the courage to ask my parents whether it was true that I had been adopted. I knew they would tell me if it was comfortable for them to talk about it. If they did not feel it was right to discuss, I would not ask them anything, even if I had a lot of questions in my head. I did not want to hurt them, because I loved my parents. They had enough to handle. I pretended nothing had happened that day.

Life returned to normal after a week. I did tell my friends in the *long-tang* the story. To my surprise, some of them already knew. They had heard their parents say so. But none of them knew who my biological parents were.

Two years later, Auntie King, my mother's sister-in-law, invited me to her home alone.

When I was small, my mother used to take me to visit Auntie King every week. She was a petite lady, a devout Buddhist, and one of the kindest-hearted women I have ever known. She was the wife of my mother's older brother. She and my mother were best friends and could chat for hours. I always sat back and listened while playing by myself quietly.

Auntie King liked to serve dessert *tang-yuan,* sticky rice flour balls filled with sweet sesame paste, when my mother and I were visiting her. Those are sticky rice flour balls filled with sweet sesame paste inside. I loved them. Always, we would talk while enjoying the treat. After visiting, the three of us usually stopped at the house down the alley to visit my godmother. Sometimes I was tired and did not want to go, but my mother always insisted.

When I turned thirteen years old, my mother started allowing me to go to Auntie King's by myself. I would take the bus to see them both.

On that day Auntie King was a little emotional. She opened her back door and welcomed me, but nervously, avoiding eye contact. We went upstairs to her apartment. She let me sit in a rosewood chair in her living room.

It was a sunny autumn afternoon. Kids were in school. The neighborhood was extra quiet. I could smell a mixture of candles and incense in the air. Auntie King kept a tiny corner shrine outside of her room to worship Buddha. I sensed something was going on and sat in the chair nervously, waiting.

I peeked at her face once, trying to find some clues, but could not.

Auntie walked to her chair, took a sip of her hot tea, and calmed herself a little bit. She started by telling me that I was adopted when I was six months old. My mother had no child by the time she was around forty years old, while my birth mother had me as the sixth baby. At that time, birth control was not a popular choice. The government encouraged people to have big families.

Auntie King was the person who arranged the adoption. As we sat in her living room, Her eyes filled with tears. Her voice was chopped with a sense of emotion. The air seemed to have stopped moving. I suddenly felt a surge of sadness in my heart, and I did not know how to control it. The tears came out and ran down my cheeks.

She passed me a clean white handkerchief. I did not know why, but I sobbed softly along with her. It might be because I felt sad about being given away or just because I did not know how to react to such a bombshell announcement.

I have never understood why my mother did not tell me about the adoption herself. I guess that she must have asked her sister-in-law to do this "challenging" job for her. She would not have the heart to explain such news to me, nor would she be able to control me if I started crying.

Although I was badly spoiled by my parents, as if they were my birth family, they also strictly trained me to behave politely and respectfully to everyone. My mother knew I would behave with Auntie King but not with her.

As a schoolteacher, Mom made only a moderate salary but helped some poor neighborhood kids when they needed it, especially paying for their medicines. Mom never mentioned any of these gestures to me, but the neighbors would tell me about her love and kindness toward their children.

The fact of my adoption was now out in the open. My conversation with Auntie King had confirmed what the Red Guards had told me during the raid. However, I decided that I belonged to my adopted family. My parents loved me with all their hearts, and we were as close as one. I loved them and could not be separated from them simply because they were my family. I did not care what people thought, only what my heart told me to do.

Then, Auntie King shocked me with another piece of news: my biological parents were the couple I called my godparents, living in the same neighborhood with her.

CHAPTER 3

GODMOTHER

Knowing that the woman down the alley was my birth mother was weird. She had always just been a 'hi and bye' neighbor to me. Now I had to take a second look at her and her whole family.

My godmother was friends with Auntie King. She was always lovely to me, but most of the time, as mentioned, I just wanted to skip the visit and go straight home after visiting Auntie King. My mother would not allow me to. I now suddenly realized why they insisted I see my godmother.

Now I had two sets of parents and two families. I had been born into this family as the youngest of four girls and two boys. I was not sure whether it was good to have two pairs of parents or not. Would it make my life too complicated?

My biological father was a mechanical engineer who graduated from the French Mechanic School (中法机械 学校), a French engineering college in Shanghai. He learned French during his college years and was fluent in it. Eventually, he became the chief engineer at a commercial printer (上海人民机器厂) and one of the recipients of the Bisheng Prize (毕升奖), the highest award in the printing trade in China, for his lifetime contribution to the industry.

I was 6 months old, with all my five siblings. (Second on left is me)

My birth mother was a beautiful and intelligent woman from a merchant's family, who grew up in Chongming, an island outside of Shanghai at the mouth of the Yangtze River, where it flows into to the East China Sea. She had always been a top student in school. Like many women in her time, she finished high school, then got married and stayed at home. She dreamed of attending the Jinling Women's College (金陵女大) in Nanjing but never got a chance to apply. Instead, she became a busy housewife with five children. Back then, most parents only supported their boys in higher education.

Her traditional Catholic school training gave my godmother beautiful penmanship, a highly respected skill in Chinese culture. I always wished I could write like her. Even staying home, she was always dressed in a matching silk scarf across her chest in qipao, the traditional Chinese dress.

Auntie King and my godmother lived about twenty minutes by rickshaw from our home. Like the yellow cabs cruising the streets today, rickshaw drivers would wander around the city hunting for customers. My mother always asked how much before getting on. She usually agreed if the ride was twenty-eight cents in Chinese yuan. Sometimes the driver asked for thirty, and my mother would keep walking. Invariably, we would soon hear the driver ride up to us and say, "OK, twenty-eight." The winner of the negotiation was always my mother.

The driver would speed us away, and I always enjoyed the rides. The seats were comfortable as we bounced along the wide boulevards and small alleyways of Shanghai, with breezes cooling us off. If it rained, the driver would put a waterproof cover over the carriage to keep us dry. Occasionally, we took the bus there. It would be a few minutes longer than the rickshaw. My mother always kept me in her sight when I was small, but at the age of thirteen, I wanted to go by myself.

The bus from my home to Auntie King's was #42. When I was thirteen years old, one day I said to my mother, "I will take the first No. 42 bus. You take the next one when it comes. I will be waiting for you at the bus stop at Auntie's house. We can then walk there together. OK?" She reluctantly agreed. The bus had two long cars with three doors. I got on to it through the front door. After three stops passed, I saw my mother emerge from the crowd of passengers at the back of the bus. I felt frustrated because she did not trust my ability to make the journey alone.

As I grew older and had my own daughter, I started understanding my mother's worry. There was no way she could find me in a huge city like Shanghai if I got off at the wrong stop.

When I was in high school, I often visited my godmother on weekends. She introduced me to sewing, tailoring, embroidering, stitching, and cooking. Perhaps surprisingly, my mother never taught me any of these things. She would buy stuff she needed ready-made in stores in a heartbeat. Godmother had five kids, and using those skills helped her to save a lot of money for the family. She believed it was a mother's job to train her girls to be perfect wives. I never understood the definition of a "perfect wife," but learning to do these home arts was fun when there was not much school work.

One evening, she in the kitchen was cleaning crabs for dinner. I passed by the sink with my eyes wide open: "Wow, they are huge! Can you show me how to cook these crabs? They look scary." I made a horrid face.

She continued what she was doing, then let me cut some easy parts of the sea animal for the preparations.

My curiosity was satisfied after ten minutes. Godmother pointed to the living room: "Go, young lady. If you are good at school, do not worry about cooking. Everybody can learn to cook, but not everybody can achieve in academics." She kicked me out of the kitchen to do my homework. Excellence in academics was always highly valued in both of my families. Today when my daughter praises me as the best cook, I realize my godmother was right about that. I learned it after I moved to the U.S. by myself. Life was the best teacher.

In the years to come, I visited my birth family more often and got to know them better. Learning new things was exciting; having brothers and sisters was a new experience. I learned to be flexible, tolerant, and cooperative with peers. Love and friendship were always in the air.

I felt as if I had known my brothers and sisters for a long time, even though we argued and fought occasionally. Maybe it was because we were blood relatives. At the end of the day, we always laughed together.

When the schools reopened more than a year after the interruption of the Cultural Revolution, the government instructed that the number of school years should be reduced and the curriculum should be simplified. I was told that my six years of middle and high school would be changed to four. The new textbook became thinner when the school reopened. A lot of the content was eliminated. The students had less homework.

The classroom culture changed. Students no longer respected their teachers. Knowledge was said to be useless. People were confused by the Revolution. They tried to understand the situation, but at time to time, they got more confused with what was right and what was wrong.

I found myself quickly getting bored in classes and after school. The libraries had limited books. Godmother kept suggesting that I learn to use her sewing machine. One day I bought a tailoring book about measuring, cutting, and sewing.

This new learning experience in my teenage years lit my curiosity and made me feel rewarded, even though it was not too easy. I used a measuring tape to measure my body, then turned the fabrics into clothes: pants, shirts, and dresses, and even curtains and pillowcases.

In everyday life, my godmother usually was the woman who knew how to do everything. One day she came to me with a piece of new fabric and said, "I can't believe that I am asking you to do this for me. I would like to use this material to make a blouse, but I don't have the paper pattern. You know how to do without it. Can you please cut it for me?" She smiled with a sense of embarrassment.

I was surprised but felt honored. "Sure. I'll be happy to."

I started measuring her chest, hip, neckline, and arms carefully, then calculated. I was a skilled tailor after those two years of self-training.

When I visited her a few weeks later, she was wearing the blouse I had cut. It was perfect on her. I was as happy as if I had passed an important test in school.

That was the only time she ever asked me for help. After my adoptive mother passed away from cancer, when I was twenty-four and in college, my godmother did beautiful sewing jobs for me when I had my daughter. Baby clothes were expensive at that time in China, but making these tiny clothes was too advanced for most young mothers, who were never trained in sewing. My godmother was a true mother to me as well.

Looking back today, I think the main reason I learned sewing well was that I was so bored due to lack of school. I would have been happy to learn anything new to avoid the disturbances of the Cultural Revolution. It was a strange time to grow up.

Among my birth siblings, I was closest to the younger of my two older brothers, Jian Ping. He was three years older than me and was always nice. The other older siblings sometimes did not take me seriously because I was too young for them. But I admired them regardless. We played chess and biked together, but what I liked most was working in the darkroom with Jian Ping.

As kids, we did not have the money for photography until my oldest brother sold some used lamps to the neighborhood junk man. He used the money to buy an old broken camera, took the lens out and turned it into a photo enlarger. When he moved out after college, we happily inherited this machine and his equipment.

We used the main bathroom to print and enlarge black and white pictures. Before starting to use the darkroom, Jian Ping would close all the windows, which were already covered by thick black paper to make the room totally dark. Then he changed the light bulb to a dim red color. Under this light, we started diluting the developing solution with water. I cut the unexposed photo paper to the correct size. Jian Ping would insert the negative into the machine, count how many seconds it took to expose it on the white paper, and then turn the enlarger light on and off quickly. As his assistant, I took the exposed paper and dipped it in the chemical solution, waiting for the picture to emerge. The process was the closest thing to a magic show for me. I never got tired of watching the photo emerge from the water. A crucial part of my job was to judge the timing of the picture paper in the water. If I let it stay in the chemical for too long, it would be too dark; if too short, the image would be too light. I honed my ability to make the right call under dim red light.

When the timing was right, I would quickly take the picture out of the water and place it into another chemical solution that stabilized the image and made it permanent. Many decades later, I showed my daughter that the photos I had developed in those early years were still as good as new. The entire process felt like creating a piece of art. It was very joyful to me and was one of the main reasons I kept going to my godmother's house. Jian Ping and I could stay in the darkroom for hours.

My godfather came home from work at six o'clock. By seven, it was family dinner time. We usually had a full table of people.

My godmother was an outstanding cook. I was always amazed by her cooking skill in putting dinner on the table for six to seven people in less than an hour. She was a person who always made difficult things look so easy.

Without long preparations, she was like a magician, putting so many delicious dishes on the table, often in half an hour. Then she would yell, "Dinner is ready, kids!" We were always hungry and would rush down the stairs. The sound of our steps on the wooden staircase felt like a rumble of thunder.

At home, I was the only child, so my mom and grand-mother always spooned the best food onto my plate. I took it for granted. But here, I had three or four siblings at dinner. I learned to eat fast before all the best dishes were gone. It was fun to have someone to compete with around the dinner table. The food tasted more delicious than when I was eating alone.

Auntie King was a good ambassador who put me between my two mothers. Since my meeting with her, I naturally became closer to my birth family. I wanted to know them more.

Having two families was not a bad thing, it turned out. I received double care and love. I would celebrate my birthday twice a year with different families. More importantly, I got good advice from both parents. However, I still believed that I belonged to my adoptive family. My mother was a woman who had a big heart. Everything seemed normal.

I was one year old.

CHAPTER 4

THE SERVANTS

As Auntie King told me, I landed in a new life without knowing it at six months old. My new family had four members: my father, 刘纬纶 (Weilun Liu), was a businessman and lawyer; my mother, 金惠宝 (Huibao Jin), was a literature teacher. Then there were my grandmother and me. A housekeeper and a butler/carpenter lived with us as well.

Our staff were like family to me. In my early childhood, our maid was Lin, a skinny widow with high cheekbones. When she smiled, she showed a glistening gold tooth in her front row of teeth. I always wanted to touch it. After my grandmother had her youngest son in the 1920s, Lin's mother was hired as a *Naima* (奶妈, or wet nurse: a woman who is hired to breastfeed another woman's baby) by my grandmother to look after her sons. Lin moved with her mother into our house so that my grandmother could have more leisure time to do things like play mahjong and entertain her friends. It was a typical lifestyle of an upper-class woman in Shanghai those times.

When Lin grew older, she helped her mother with light work around the house. She looked happy with a big smile. Sadly, her personal story was not as sweet as her smile. Before Lin was seven years old, both her parents passed away from illnesses. My grandmother had great sympathy for her and kept her with our family after her mother died.

In Lin's early twenties, she met a young man from her village and married. The couple lived in a town near the city of Wuxi. One day, her husband was found drowned in a river nearby. He died while Lin was pregnant with their first baby. Many years later, when her only son was ready for his wedding in the 1960s, my grandmother instructed my father and Uncle Wei Tong to pay for his wedding banquet and the expenses of building their new house.

My grandmother called it a loan to the groom, knowing they would almost never be able to pay it back. In traditional Chinese philosophy, people should only help people who would help themselves but not give them charity in a way that will make them lazy. That was the reason my grandmother called it a "loan." It was a huge favor to a peasant at that time.

I always remember Lin as a loyal member of our household. When the Cultural Revolution pounded China, my family suffered humiliation. All our money was taken away with no warning. My father's salary was cut to a fraction. None of our relatives dared to visit us.

In the week before Chinese New Year, Lin would appear at the back door and sneak into our kitchen quietly, bringing us a big leg of country ham she'd preserved, live chickens from her backyard, and sticky rice flour, which was a must-have for my grandmother during the New Year.

Seeing Lin was one of the happiest times for my mother and grandmother during those dark years. It was as if they were welcoming a long-lost daughter back home.

During the coldest winter days of the Revolution, Lin's visits to us were not only about the delicious foods we desperately needed; they also brought precious love that warmed my family's lonely hearts.

As a child, I heard Lin say over and over that they must repay the loan, but neither my father nor my uncle ever brought it up until Lin's only son died of kidney disease in his late forties.

Children dying before their parents is the saddest thing anywhere in the world, but the tragedy was made worse in rural China, a country where grown children were the only financial resource for aging parents. Lin retired to her home in the later 1980s. A few years later, we learned she had hanged herself.

No one really knew why she ended her life like this. During her last visit, I overheard her telling my father that her daughter-in-law did not welcome her to her own home and spread rumors in the village that Lin brought bad luck to the people living around her.

This was the most tragic story I have ever experienced and one of the innumerable examples of the darkness of feudal Chinese society's influence over thousands of years when ignorance and superstitions dominated daily life for people who were poor and uneducated. I miss Lin as a loving woman and a kind nanny.

My family also had a live-in butler who worked as a carpenter. He was a single man in his forties, always smiling but taciturn. His skills as a craftsman were well known in our neighborhood. A lot of beautifully designed furniture our family had was from his hands and made to his own design. It lasted well and its classic oriental style was never out of fashion.

Everyone called him Lao Si, meaning "The Old #4" in Chinese, despite the fact that he had his own name: Mr. Gao. It could be that he was the fourth child in his family, but I had never heard about his siblings. Or it could be that he was the fourth employee in our house when he got hired.

In China, it is acceptable to name someone by a number. Especially in the lower-working class, a person's name was not important, so it was not uncommon to go by a number that was convenient for their employer to recall. In the old times, many parents even named their children after numbers. When it came as part of the culture, it could be powerful and permanent as a mountain last forever. Everybody accepted the practice as is.

The Eastern and Western cultural philosophies could be so different. One person's poison would be another's treasure. When I was a teenager, the first time I read Victor Hugo's novel *Les Misérables*, it struck me that Jean Valjean felt so insulted when the policeman called him by his prison number instead of his name when he found him escaping. It hit his soul and hit mine too. However, Lao Si was happy with his name, "#4."

Even though Lao Si was not married and had no kids, he had a tender heart toward neighborhood children, and they loved him too. One of the most enjoyable things of the day for him was watching me show off my new dances learned in kindergarten. He always grinned and gave me big applause when I finished it. But he never hugged or kissed because he understood we were on different societal levels of life. Lao Si eventually married when he was in his late fifties, leaving our house. He came back to visit us like a family friend with his new wife. We were all happy for him.

CHAPTER 5

MY CHILDHOOD HOME

My childhood home was located in a long alley, with a stone frame door and three floors. Walking through the tall black wooden front door, you would find a high-walled courtyard where my grandmother planted flowers all year round.

Entered through the wall of tall glass doors, the living room had a high ceiling and beautiful blue-and-white ceramic tiles floor. It made me think of the traditional Spanish tiles. The blue-and-white color pattern was my grandmother's favorite. I thought they might have been imported from Europe in colonial times.

On a hot summer day, I loved to walk on these tiles barefoot and feel the instant cool from the earth directly beneath. The traditional style of dark rosewood armchairs and tea tables contrasted with the warm color of flowering wallpaper, making the room welcoming. Traditional Chinese brush paintings hung on the walls and there was a piano sitting on the west side of the room. It belonged to Uncle Wei Zuo's wife, an outstanding pianist. They rushed to Taiwan in 1949 when the Communists came.

In the morning, the sun would cover the dark piano, making it shine like a mirror. When I came down the stairs to have breakfast in the dining room, it was always the first piece of furniture to say *good morning* to me. Altogether, it made a formal classic Shanghai living room in the 1960s.

Our kitchen was toward the back of the house, separated by a wooden door. It was the busiest room every day around mealtimes. I loved to go there and knew that as soon as I saw and smelled the food, I would feel hungry. If my mother were cooking, she would stop me and put a tasty piece of goodness into my mouth and wait for the expression on my face. I always gave a big smile and nodded back to her. That would make my day.

Every morning at dawn, when the entire world was still sleeping, my grandmother would get up, open one side of the heavy black doors, and sweep the ground until it was spotless. Then she would go to the kitchen to prepare breakfast for the

Dad at the front door of our old house that was demolished in the 1990s.

whole family. When I woke up, the house always smelled so good from the food. I still miss the aroma of the scallion pancakes.

My parents and I lived in the second-floor front bedrooms while my grandmother occupied the smaller bedroom in the back of the house with a large loft built by Lao Si. Uncle and Aunt lived on the third floor, which was not big but cozy and private.

In the '90s, the government tore the whole area down to build commercial high-rises. It broke my father's heart to be forced out. He loved his home, which had a lot of happy and sad memories. However, there was nothing anyone could do about it. To be Chinese, you must obey.

On one crisp, sunny spring day in the 2000s, I was visiting my dad in Shanghai from the U.S. Spring usually meant wet and cool in Shanghai. If it was a sunny day, people must plan to do something outdoors.

Dad was in his early nineties, living in a new apartment with a live-in housekeeper. Sitting in a chair in his study, he called me in.

He was looking at a black and white picture of our family's old house. "It is a beautiful day today, isn't it? Would you like to take me to the Four Seasons Hotel in the city center?"

"Why do we want to go to a hotel, Dad?" I was surprised by his request.

Dad lifted his sagged eyelid, looking through a window to the bright green tree branches outside, and said calmly, "That is where our home used to be."

"Oh! Is it a Four Seasons now?" I asked, having not heard the news.

"Yes, I was told that they tore down all the neighborhood buildings and put a big hotel there. I want to take a look at that place again. Can you take me there?"

"Of course, let's go." I would love to see it too. Quickly, I called a cab.

In the taxi, Dad was busy looking around the streets we passed by.

"What are you looking for, Dad?" I asked.

"I can't believe this area has changed so much! I don't recognize where we are now anymore," he said. Dad had lived in Shanghai for eighty years. Every inch of the city was in his head. He could close his eyes and make turns. Now, he got lost.

"Yes, it looks like a totally different city," I agreed, my jaw dropping in shock. The neighborhood used to have all two-storied traditional stone gate dwellings with some stores on the first floor. Now every building was at least twenty floors high. All the little stores I used to walk by from school were gone.

During that short taxi ride, Dad tried to map what was in his memories onto what he was seeing out of the car window. When we arrived, there were a few people on the streets, but all my neighbors were gone.

A modern box-style tall hotel building was sitting in the location of my childhood home, where my daughter and I were born, my mother and grandmother passed away, and my dad lived for forty more years. The traditional row homes, the narrow alley, the courtyards, the people I used to play with, and even the beautiful French plane sidewalk trees were all gone. I had no idea where my neighbors had moved to. It was a farewell without a goodbye. I felt a sense of loss and sadness.

Dad looked around and smiled as if a long-time wish had been fulfilled that day. Sitting in his wheelchair, he asked me to take photos with him outside the Four Seasons hotel. We did not go in.

My father was a man with many thoughts but few words. On that day, he did not say a word about the changes, but I know he had mixed feelings in his heart that he preferred not to be discussed. This was the last time I visited this site. Shanghai became a city of tall new buildings with very few historical quarters. When I went back to see, I missed the sense of belonging.

My childhood home is gone, but it will live in my memories forever.

Dad visiting our family's old home address which now is the Four Seasons Hotel.

CHAPTER 6

GRANDMOTHER

Buddhism has been the major religion for over 4,000 years in China, surviving even under the Communist Party's rule. My grandmother was a believer. She strictly followed specific Buddhist diet rules: No food from animals, such as meat, fish, egg, and even dairy products, on every 1st and the 15th of the month in the lunar calendar. On these dates, my grandmother allowed herself to eat only vegetables. This made my mother's life a little complicated. I often heard her apologizing to Grandmother: "I am so sorry, Mom, I forgot to buy some more vegetables for you today. Let me go back to the market again." Grandmother would say, "Oh, don't. I am OK. Don't worry about it." But my mother would be unhappy for the whole day.

As the oldest son's wife in a traditional extended family, my mother had a handful of duties. It was a uniquely challenging position. She must be the role model for younger members of the household, like the wives of my father's younger brothers. At the same time, she also had to serve my grandmother and my father well. Although my mother was supposed to be the boss to manage all the family affairs, she did not. My father was ultimately in charge. He was a general manager at work and a boss at home as well. Dad liked to handle money matters himself. Every morning, he would give my mother a certain amount of money for the food market and he controlled the household budgeting in detail. I never heard my mother complain about it. She put everything inside her and tried to be a model wife, mother, and daughter-in-law all at once.

Grandmother lost most of her teeth in her seventies, so her whole mouth was full of dentures. She did not like her false teeth and hardly ever wore them, which meant she could only consume soft food.

In the meantime, my mother invented ying-yang (阴阳) rice. When cooking rice for the whole family, she put the pot unevenly on the heat so that half the pot of rice was covered in too much water, becoming softer than the other half. The drier half was for us: we had teeth. My mother's invention left everybody at the dinner table satisfied.

Auntie King always had sympathy and admired my mother's complicated role under my grandma's and my father's supervision. She told me numerous times that my mom was the best traditional Chinese wife, mother, and daughter-in-law. Mother was not happy with her role in our family. I could not understand totally what Auntie King meant, but I sensed it when my mom got in a bad mood toward me.

One of the behaviors I hate in Chinese culture is that beating children is tolerated by society. It was regarded as a parent's job to discipline their kids. Once in a while, my mother could get mad at me for something. She would pull me to the second-floor bedroom and beat me with her hand.

It was the most horrifying moment! I was about five to seven years old and did not have the strength to fight back, only crying for Auntie in the third-floor apartment to save me.

I would yell at the top of my lungs, "Teer… help…!" This was Auntie's nickname I had made up. When I was learning to talk, I had a problem pronouncing "Auntie"; instead, I could only say "Teer." Now I was desperate for help; her nickname came out as the first word from my mouth. Teer would fly as fast as she could from anywhere in the house to my rescue.

Auntie was a product of Western education. She could not be tolerant of such things happening in front of her. Quick as lightning, she would arrive within a minute and separate us. Mom would still be angry and out of breath. I was traumatized and crying. But Auntie never criticized my mom for doing it to me. After a fight like this, my mother would forget it after a day, and I forgave her unconditionally until the next time she beat me.

I told myself that I would never hit my child. It was a nightmare. Now that I am older, I believe that my mother could have been under pressure due to extended family life. I did not understand this at the time. My mother always tried to be the best, but my grandmother had her own rules and was the queen. In an old-fashioned extended family, my mother had to keep her sad feelings inside her. Auntie King explained to me that if my mother was unhappy, it was mainly because of the conflicts with Grandmother and the difficulty fitting into the family.

When I was a teenager, I read the great classic Chinese novel *The Dream of the Red Mansion* and started understanding what a role in a traditional family meant to a woman. I told myself that I wanted to live as a free spirit when I grew up. I didn't have to be rich, but I must have the freedom to do what

I wanted. However, what my mother felt in her heart remains a mystery to me to this day.

Every Chinese New Year's Eve, Grandmother would lead us in a sacrifice to our ancestors. She and my mother would cook a lot of food: hot and cold dishes, soup, and rice, filling up the little blue and white china winecups with special Chinese wine. Grandmother would cover the mirrors, light candles, and put a soft pad on the floor. She would tell me not to touch the table because the ancestors were coming. As the youngest in the room, I was always the first one to kneel on the pad, praying to all my ancestors, whom I had never met, for blessing us. After the ceremony was done, we stood to the side to wait for the spirits to finish their dinner. I was always hungry and bored, wondering if the invisible ghost guests were really in the room. There were times when the adults turned away and, with nobody watching me, I touched the table quickly and expected black smoke to come out or something even worse. But nothing ever happened. I never believed it. However, this ancestor ceremony is widely observed in Chinese families even today.

Later in life, I found it did not matter if my ancestors came or not. The ceremony helped us heal the heart-breaking sadness of losing our loved ones. It was a reunion, an effective treatment for healing.

Grandmother was the eldest among us, so she was regarded as the highest authority according to the culture. Everyone obeyed her absolutely. I never heard my parents ever argue with Grandmother. It was said that when my older cousins made Grandmother angry, they would be made to kneel down until she forgave them. Somehow, I was the only one who fought with her all the time. I still don't know why I could behave like this. Maybe my parents spoiled me; perhaps I was a defiant rebel by nature.

One day, after arguing with my grandmother, I was still uneasy. My uncle came to calm me down. He took me to another room, just the two of us. To my surprise, Uncle looked me in the eye: "Do not fight with your grandma. She did not have the chance to get a good education." He stopped here for a second, then continued, "It was not because she didn't want to learn, nor that she could not achieve. Her family could not afford it." I listened quietly and did not say a word. What did he mean? My head was spinning. I had been taught to obey all the authorities since the day I was born. Arguing with my grandmother was unacceptable—I knew the rules too well, though I did not want to follow them. Now Uncle's words implied that it was OK to disagree with Grandmother, though I must understand where she came from. I felt confused, but a new confidence was growing inside me: As a child, I could have a voice too. I only needed to be more respectful of Grandmother.

At that moment, I told myself I would behave and never trouble my uncle. In the old society's eye, he educated me with a philosophy that was not rooted in Chinese culture and did not fit into standard practice. However, these kinds of talks happened almost every day in our home, though they were scarce in most Chinese families. In the traditional value of culture, a child should never criticize an adult. Questioning them should not be encouraged.

My uncle did not teach me to blindly "obey" but to think independently and critically. It impacted my whole life. I learned to be more tolerant and forgive people I disagreed with, including my grandmother.

At the time of my adoption, my parents had several options for choosing a baby. It was my grandmother who loved me at first sight. People believed it was fate. I hope she had no regrets that she picked up a rebellious baby by mistake.

My grandmother was a super-intelligent woman born into a farmer's family in the countryside of the city of Wuxi. She never received a single day of school and was illiterate. In her childhood, only boys would attend school, especially in rural areas.

My grandfather was an entrepreneur, fluent in English, who passed away before the age of thirty from an unknown disease. Grandmother raised her three boys—then three, six, and nine years old—by herself and never remarried. She managed to send her sons to law, music, and medical schools, respectively, with the money from her late husband's business (精益眼镜公司), which was once the largest optician franchise in China.

As I remember it, my father was always out during the day, working as a manager in a government-owned company after the Communist Party took over all private business ownership in 1955.[2]

---

2   Public–Private Partnership (公私合营). At the beginning of 1956, there was a climax of socialist transformation across the country, and capitalist industry and commerce achieved a public–private partnership in the whole industry. The state's redemption of capitalist private shares changed to a "fixed-rate system," with a flat annual interest rate of 5%. The means of production were uniformly allocated and used by the state. In addition to the fixed interest rates, the capitalists no longer exercised their functions and powers as capitalists and gradually transformed themselves into self-sufficient laborers. In September 1966, the expiration of the fixed-rate period, the public–private partnership finally turned into socialist ownership.

One of Dad's hobbies was singing in the Peking Opera, in Shanghai, 1940s.

As a little kid, I constantly felt Dad was like the light bulb in the refrigerator—when I needed him, I knew where to look for him, but I never understood what he was doing there when the door was closed. After coming home, he often spent more time talking to people on the phone or writing in his study. He loved me dearly and bought me a lot of toys and books, but he hardly had time to play with me.

I often heard my dad talk about his younger brother Wei Zuo and his family. Uncle Wei Zuo was the first violin payer for the Symphony Orchestra of Shanghai (上海工部局交响乐队) in the 1940s. From our family photos and my father's stories, I knew he was a handsome and brilliant man and a close friend of the Chinese First Lady, Madame Chiang Soong May Ling, the wife of the then President of the Republic of China, Mr. Chiang Kai-Shek. That friendship later gave my father lots of trouble during the Cultural Revolution. Uncle Wei. Zuo's wife, Aunt Jin-Nong, was a talented pianist and an excellent cook. They and their three daughters moved to Taiwan in 1949 when the Communists took over mainland China and the Kuomintang government fled to the island. There were no diplomatic relationships or mail service between the two sides of the Taiwan Strait, and we lost contact with Uncle Wei Zuo and his family.

Twenty years was an unthinkably long period for a mother and son's separation. My grandmother missed Uncle Wei Zuo every day but never allowed her feelings to show. When she was old and very ill, I once heard my father asking her whether there was anything that she wanted to talk about. Did she miss her son in Taiwan? Grandmother raised her hand to stop Dad from speaking further. I watched as a trickle of tears quietly seeped down her cheeks. She died at home at the age of ninety-two.

The goodbye between a mother and son in 1949 became a forever farewell in life. Later in 1979, we learned that Uncle Wei Zuo had worked as the general manager of the Grand Hotel in Taipei until he retired. Their three daughters attended graduate schools in the U.S. After retirement, Uncle Wei Zuo moved to California to join his children and grandchildren happily ever after. I wish my grandmother could hear this and smile in heaven.

During the raid on my parents' house, the Red Guards found a suitcase that Uncle Wei Zuo had left in our attic in 1949. Grandmother had prohibited anybody from touching it because it was her favorite son's private belongings.

When the Red Guards opened it, they found a picture of Chiang Kai-Shek holding one of their children, along with a pistol in the suitcase! This was a big crime against my father when the Red Guards found them. They questioned my father many times. Grandmother was brave and told the Red Guards that it was her idea not to let her other sons open the suitcase. She was protecting her Wei Zuo's privacy. That was why my father honestly did not know the contents of these suitcases. Her attitude persuaded the Red Guards to believe her story and they finally let my father go.

CHAPTER 7

KINDERGARTEN

Despite my rebellious streak, my grandmother said I was an easy kid to raise. I rarely got sick or brought trouble to my parents. But time passed quickly. Grandmom said it was as if she had put a clean sheet on the clothesline, and in the blink of an eye, when she took the sheet off, I was already a big girl.

When I was five, my mother decided to send me to kindergarten to socialize with other kids. She was afraid that I was lonely at home, where, as an only child, I was always looking for adults to play with.

Most of the children in my neighborhood were watched by their grandparents while their mothers went to work. Kindergarten education was neither mandatory nor free. My grandmother did not allow me to play with some of the kids in the *long-tang* because she believed that I could learn bad behaviors from them. Even with my giant pile of toys in the corner of our courtyard, my mother watched as I got bored and continued to yearn to go out to play. She decided kindergarten was good for me.

In the '60s, education was an added expense for families, who had to pay tuition for K–12 schooling. Since the average worker's income was low, even small tuition fees would eat into their living expenses, especially when a family had five to seven kids. But for impoverished families, the schools offered reduced tuition or waived it entirely.

Regardless of whether rich or poor, there were almost no families I had ever known who refused to pay for their children's tuition. No matter how difficult their life was, education was always the top priority for Chinese parents.

There was a well-known quote from Confucianism: *The scholar is superior to all others in society.* These values were deeply rooted in China until the Cultural Revolution in 1966. Chairman Mao sharply criticized Confucianism. Many editorial articles with the same voices were published in the Party's newspaper, *People's Daily.* The newspaper was the government's mouthpiece to tell the country what they should think.

The movement against Confucianism shook the ideological and philosophical roots of Chinese history tremendously. The change of values in people's minds confused old and young. It created the most significant turmoil in society. People did not know what path to follow. They lost their moral standards and were disoriented. China went crazy in all directions during the Cultural Revolution.

The Young Women's Christian Association ran my kindergarten. The Party never said religion was prohibited but also never encouraged it. Since the 1949 liberation, all religious organizations in China had been independent of their counterparts in the rest of the world. For example, Catholic churches were separate from the Vatican. The kindergarten had changed its name to the Young Women's Association Kindergarten, dropping the word 'Christian'. No matter what it was called, the kindergarten was prestigious and difficult to get into. My mother had to ask a favor of a friend of the school's principal to get me registered, and I had to pass an I.Q. test.

I liked my new life in kindergarten. Every morning as soon as I said goodbye to my mother at the school door, I immediately jumped into my friends' group. While playing, we were taught math and other skills in class. The teacher would put three paper ducks on a soft blackboard, then add two more, asking us to count to 1, 2, 3, 4, 5, and so on. Every kid learned this quickly while we were playing. The kindergarten taught us addition and subtraction before first grade.

Quickly, I made many new friends in my class, and the only difficult thing for me was afternoon napping. Every day after lunch, the teacher's assistant put bedding mats and sheets on the floor. All the kids lay down for a two-hour nap, alternating in the direction we slept, but I could never fall asleep easily. Feeling bored, I would start disturbing the next kid but one. As a result, I always got punished at the end of the napping period. Sometimes, the teachers would put me in a dark room for "re-napping." After I had been there for five minutes, an assistant would come and "rescue" me. She took me to see my teacher, asking me to say, "I promise I will never do it again." I repeated after her reluctantly. Then it was the end of the story. I was forgiven every time, but I remained the "bad napping girl" for the rest of my kindergarten days.

Although I loved my school and friends there, waiting for my mother to pick me up was always the happiest time of the afternoon. I missed her for the whole day. When my mother and I reached home, another task was waiting for me: a piano lesson. I wanted to run in the *long-tang*, play with my friends, not start another class after a whole day of school. But this was my parents' plan for me. My piano teacher, Ms. Su, was a petite lady with straight gray hair. She was very kind but boring. I never liked playing the piano.

Every afternoon, I started to practice around four o'clock. My buddies in the *long-tang* were waiting and peeking from our front door. I kept looking at them while putting my fingers on the keyboard. I was miserable. Eventually, I made my mother give up and allow me to quit. That was my first taste of victory over obedience.

Shortly after I started kindergarten, the Great Chinese Famine began. It was one of the most significant man-made disasters in Chinese history, killing an estimated 45 million people as it swept across the country between 1959 and 1961.[3] Early on, many people starved to death in the rural areas. Soon it even reached big cities like Shanghai.

I was 4 years old in kindergarten.

---

3   See "Mao's Great Leap to Famine," Frank Dikötter, December 15, 2010, *New York Times.*

Food was rationed, with every city resident only allowed to consume food within the set quotas. These quotas were enforced through coupons distributed by the government. Meat, fish, sugar, cooking oil, rice, and even cigarettes and fabric for clothing all had their own coupons. As far back as I can remember, the program was for cities only.

I remember that the monthly rice and flour quota for one person was 29 Jin (市斤) per month, a Chinese measurement equaling about 31 pounds. People working in manual labor jobs would have a higher allowance, around 35 pounds. Today, we may say 31 pounds of rice in a month is more than enough for anyone, but in those years, rice was the primary food, supplemented by vegetables. Very few meats, seafood, sugar, or cooking oil were available, so people had to consume a lot of carbohydrates, like rice and wheat, to keep them energized.

On paper, the quota system was a smart way to feed a vast population: Nobody would starve to death, but nobody would be able to waste food either. It effectively prevented selling goods in black markets because no one could monopolize particular interests in a big city like Shanghai. I must give the government a thumbs up. The problem was that the whole nation was starving and a much larger food supply was needed.

When I first arrived in the U.S. in the '80s, I was surprised to see many overweight people using government assistance food coupons. Why did they need more food while they were already overweight? I thought poor and skinny must be a universal combination. In my whole life, the only poor people I had seen in China were skinny. That was one of the most significant cultural shocks to me as a newcomer.

I often heard my mother complain about my expensive kindergarten tuition. On top of that, she had to pay coupons to the school for my daily lunch. At the same time, she was pleased that the school provided me with both good education and good nutrition. Every day at lunch, the kindergarten children had to take calcium and fish oil supplements. I hated the huge horse pill of calcium, always spitting it out when the teacher turned around and throwing it into the toilet. At the end-of-year physical, my mother wondered why my calcium level was slightly lower than everyone else's. Only I knew. However, I could never escape the fish oil because it was put into my mouth directly. The taste was very fishy! Cow milk was hard to get. We drank soymilk everyday instead.

When my mother picked me up in the afternoons, she liked to ask what I had eaten at school. Often it was fried rice with eggs as lunch and crispy sugar pancakes as an afternoon snack. Then my mother would smile and say that I was a lucky kid to have those. For today's children, this is nothing close to a treat. But then, at home, they did not have as many food choices.

I never knew how my mother managed to put food on the dinner table every day, because there were shortages of all kinds of food. Even vegetable oil was hard to come by. When she prepared our meals, my mother would boil vegetables and then put a little heated oil on the top to make them look and taste better. Frying food was rare and a luxurious thing. Meat or fish was usually only available during the Chinese New Year with holiday coupons. It was as if the whole nation was on a strict diet: vegetables only, limited sugar and oil, no fried food. Many children and adults were too skinny and suffered from malnutrition. People congratulated each other if they managed to put on weight. "Wow, you are fat!" "Hey, I haven't seen you for a while. You gained weight. Congratulations!" were popular flattering greetings then.

At home with my mom, I hardly felt any lack of food. My father's friend Mr. Chou, the manager of the Hong Kong optical company branch who was not forced to join the Public–Private Partnership, often mailed us packages of sugar and cooking oil via the post. My mother was always so joyful when she received these rectangular tins, though she kept her excitement private because neighbors did not have the same opportunities to enjoy it.

Once in a while, my grandmother would take my mother and me out to a feast. At lunchtime, she would call a three-wheeled rickshaw to our house. We jumped on, heading straight to the restaurant. Often the restaurant was only one block away; I guess the rickshaw ride was Grandmother's strategy to get rid of nosy neighbors. Not causing others to be jealous was one of the keys to protecting ourselves under these circumstances. People could not know where we were heading to.

I grew up in a society where religion was not encouraged and was outwardly regarded as supernatural. However, I frequently saw people practicing religion in private. Auntie King had a particular corner of her room for worship, as did many Chinese.

Sometimes, I heard my uncle Wei Tong talk about Christian beliefs at home. He and his wife had both graduated from Yenching University, a Christian school, and the Peking

Union Medical College. Sometimes, my uncle introduced me to Christian stories and we discussed them. They were interesting and for the first time they opened my mind to how people in other parts of the world thought. I realized there were beautiful cultures other than Chinese. They were fascinating and lovely.

As a child, I listened to these stories with great curiosity, as if seeing a colorful new light from another world, but I was not sure whether it was a real light, whether I should believe it.

Under the Communist empire throughout my whole life in China, I was told in school by the government not to believe in religion. But I somehow agreed with many Christian principles, such as loving your neighbors—I loved my friends in the *longtang*. However, I was not sure if I was convinced by the idea of Christian forgiveness yet.

The Chinese authorities always told people to strike back without mercy, not to forgive if someone harmed you, and to hate all enemies forever. These two different principles fought in my head, but at the end of the day, they sat alongside each other in my heart. I never decided my views toward religion and am still searching for answers.

In everyday life, the government encouraged its citizens to report other people's "wrongdoing." I believe this kind of brainwashing education poisoned the kindnesses of human nature. People were told they were supposed to be loyal only to the Party. Since I learned to walk and talk, my parents always warned me that I should never discuss certain topics—particularly political topics—outside our family. I followed this rule as a child and adult every day in China.

I was struck when I visited Germany a few years ago by finding similarities with China in the DDR Museum in Berlin, with its exhibitions displaying life in former East Germany. As a Chinese proverb says, *"All crows are equally black under the sun, no matter where they come from."* It was the same Communist ruling in different countries, cultures, races, and continents. There was the feeling of always being under surveillance by the government. I felt like I was listening to different songs with similar melodies in the DDR Museum. A dictator's principle was like a crow's feather: always black, even if they came from far away.

In our neighborhood, some families with many kids lived in crowded tenement houses. When I played with their children, I sometimes felt their jealousy toward me because we had so much more space. I learned to be low-key about what happened in our household.

One day, a girl complained that my family lived in a whole house while her seven family members squeezed into a tiny apartment. Her brother and sisters crammed together in a small loft to sleep at home. When the Shanghai summer heatwave struck, they had to move their dinner table outside into the *long-tang*. On some sweltering nights, the family slept under the open sky. I told my grandmother about this. Grandmother was not happy and asked me not to play with her. I thought Grandmother was being prejudiced, so I still went to play with her.

Not long after that, an official from the government housing department came to my home and told my parents that we must give away a room for others who needed it. No one could say no to the authorities, so we had to give up the extra room. Our house was a single-family home and not meant to be rented piecemeal. Grandmother decided to give away the kitchen, which had a separate entrance, so our family could keep our privacy. The black front door became our only entrance. In the meantime, we converted a small room next to our living room into the kitchen. My family, my uncle and auntie shared it as the only kitchen for the next eight years, until the hot summer night in 1966 when the Red Guards arrived at our door.

CHAPTER 8

A PERFECT STUDENT

Before I knew it, I had reached elementary school age. On the first day of school, I got up early. Mom took the time to do my hair in twin braids with large pink polka dot bows on each side. It was a beautiful, sunny, cool day in September. My elementary school was five minutes' walk from my home. The same school my cousins attended. It was an elegant two-story red-brick building with a large Western-style white balcony overlooking the big playing field where students had morning stretch exercises and the flag ceremony. I was excited!

My first-grade teacher was a petite woman in her fifties with neat gray hair down her back. She always had an easy smile on her face. The class had fifty kids, which was the standard size for Shanghai schools. Each two students shared a wooden desk and a bench. My classroom was very bright, with tall glass windows and white walls.

One day before class was dismissed, the teacher called me to help her pass along some handouts to everyone. I was happy to help. By the end of the week, she said, "Can you help me to do it every day after class?" I was not sure but nodded OK.

After school, I took the students across the traffic lights safely. It was an honor to get this job—the adults trusted me. It is said by the Chinese that the best way to show respect for a person is to do what they ask you to do. The teacher was in a very respected position in society. No one is supposed to question a teacher's words, even parents. I learned the rules as a first grader, but I hated having to obey.

In the classroom, all seats were assigned and could not be changed. I often sat next to a problem kid for a whole semester because the teacher believed that I could be a "role model" to him (it was usually a boy) and could help him. I wouldn't say I liked this job, and I used a pencil and a knife to draw a line halfway along the desk as a border. No one was supposed to cross it. That line served to preserve the peace with my desk-mate.

Every day after school, it was "Small Group" time, held at one student's home to do homework together for an hour. We were divided into four students per group and would play together after our task.

Even during summer vacation, we still had homework and Small Group activities. It was usually hosted by a family with a large house and an adult at home to supervise. My home was always the perfect candidate. Grandmother seated us in the covered courtyard outside, even on rainy days, keeping the house clean and neat.

When we arrived at my house after school, we were invariably hungry. Grandmother always had some cookies or candies ready for us to eat. We would finish them in minutes before starting to do our homework.

During the hour, whoever had questions could ask each other. I learned to help people and get help from peers on assignments. I also learned how to make people listen to me. The teacher put me in charge of our Small Group. Occasionally, she would pop in to check if we were really studying or just playing. Before our session was dismissed, it was my job to inspect everyone's homework, ensuring they had completed the job. When we finished everything, we were dismissed and could play in the *long-tang*. That would be our happy time of the day.

One afternoon, my teacher came in suddenly and greeted my grandmother, then started to check our homework assignments. She turned around to question one of the girls: "Is this your own work?"

The girl lowered her eyes and said nothing. The teacher peeked at me unhappily. Yes, the girl copied my homework. I knew it, but I let her do. Sometimes I got frustrated tutoring. However, it was not only wrong for her but wrong for me as well. I felt such a sense of embarrassment. I never let it happen again.

The Small Group sessions were an excellent approach to teaching pupils to study outside school and in a safe environment with "free" adult supervision. It was a brilliant example of teaching kids about leadership, helping and learning from their peers, and being honest with school work at no cost.

I am surprised that this method is not more widely acknowledged or promoted outside China. Our peer-to-peer tutoring sessions taught me responsibility and leadership skills at a very young age, which benefited me throughout my life.

Looking at the thousand years of long Chinese history, whether in modern society or the dynastic era, academic excellence was always one of the highest values recognized by all ethnic groups, among rich and poor alike. Those values inspired many young hearts from less privileged families to achieve elite levels, which forever changed their lives.

After moving to the U.S., I witnessed many Chinese kids from lower-income families doing well in school even though their immigrant parents had never finished high school. Some of their parents worked in the restaurant business and were home at midnight. These kids might not be at the top of their class, but they were never far behind. I often wondered how they could achieve so much success in a foreign environment without adult supervision. That was the value of the Confucianism their parents seeded into their hearts: the belief that education and hard work would bring success. They were thrilled by the freedom in this country.

From time to time, I asked myself: if I had been born and grown up in a different place, would I have become a different person? This was always the big question in my head.

When I was in second grade, I discovered the world of books. One day my teacher called me into her office and gave me an application form to the Shanghai Children's Library. It was a big honor for a child that age to have a library card, especially from the best children's library in the country. The library was sponsored by the foundation of Ms. Soong Ch'ing-ling, the wife of the late founding father of modern China, Mr. Sun Yat-sen. Teachers gave library cards only to the students who were doing well academically, in order to encourage them to continue to learn. Reading for pleasure was not as important as academia in my teacher's eyes.

That library card opened an incredible door for me. For the first time, I found that there was a whole new world within books that I wanted to explore. The library was in a red-brick mansion with a beautiful garden. Reading quietly there was a privilege for an average kid like me. I could totally lose myself in the book's story. Many times, I lifted my eyes from a book, looked around the reading room and asked myself where in the world I was.

My home was a fifteen-minute walk from the library. Often, I couldn't wait to read a new book I had just borrowed and started while I walked home. Sometimes I was concentrating so hard on the story, I did not notice that I had dropped my library card on the street. Several times, strangers hand-delivered it to my home. I still remember my ID picture on the card: a short-haired me with a red scarf around my neck. That scarf showed that I was a member of the Chinese Young Pioneer Organization, an organization for young children. It started in third grade with teacher recommendations. We were all required to apply. The red scarf was a sign of a good kid in the eyes of China's Communist society.

Reading gave me great pleasure and had a significant impact throughout my life. I could lose myself in books for hours and forget to eat or play. It impacted my decision to major in library science in college.

Every week I visited the children's library at least once. I enjoyed my library card for years, until the summer of 1966, when the Cultural Revolution started and all libraries were restricted to lending only Mao's books. With nothing to borrow, I struggled to maintain my membership in good standing.

One day, a librarian asked me if I did not like to read.

I looked at her with disbelief. How could anyone ask me such a stupid question? Didn't she know this library only had Mao's books?

However, I understood that removing patrons' unused cards was her job. Sadly, I gave my beloved library card to her. I did not think I would ever set foot inside that place again.

Fifty years later, when I revisited Shanghai, I passed by that mansion again. Holding my heartbeats, I walked into the garden to seek my childhood memories. The building was still the same, nicely maintained. But the beloved funder, Madame Sun Yat-sen, had passed away; now only her statue was sitting in the garden green. The library was still so close to my heart in my dreams but so far away as a strange place to me now. My childhood heaven was gone forever.

During those confusing years of the Cultural Revolution, even classic novels were prohibited, only Mao's books filled the shelves of libraries, bookstores, and classrooms... The brutal actions of the Red Guards forced people to be quiet for their safety.

But even in those darkest days of the Revolution, I had friends who had the ability to steal library books and pass them around. Next door to us lived an art student a few years older than me. He often lent me some great 18th- and 19th-century European novels, like *War and Peace, Anna Karenina, Eugénie Grandet, The Gadfly*. I usually only got a two- or three-day loan for a book of over 600 pages. I read it as fast as I could, day and night, then exchanged it for another.

My mother had strict nine o'clock bedtime for me, but I always had difficulty falling asleep on her schedule. One fun thing for me to pass the time in my dark bedroom was to put my ear to the wall, listening to my aunt chatting with my mother in the next room. They would talk about friends or gossip about acquaintances. One night, I heard my aunt ask my mother in a serious tone, "Hey, do you know what kind of book the kid was reading? *The Red and the Black!*"

That was a 19th-century French novel, one of my all-time favorites. Of course, it was prohibited by the authorities. That overheard conversation alerted me. If my book were confiscated, I would never get another one from the same guy. I began to hide my books more carefully from the adults. I was like a runner thirsty for water, a plant eager for the sun, and I kept reading. Thanks to many great Chinese foreign-language translators, I finished piles and piles of literature in my early teenage years. Believe it or not, I did not feel lonely or bored when school was closed. It was one of the happiest times in my life.

CHAPTER 9

NEVER GIVE UP

The Cultural Revolution changed my life and my views of the world forever. My father was a well-respected businessman who suddenly became an "enemy of the people." Overnight, I went from a perfect student to a born "bad-blood" child because of my upper-class family background. It confused and depressed me as a teenager.

Besides that, there was so much news about people committing suicide. Many of them were famous scholars, businessmen, teachers. They got beaten by the Red Guards. Some died under their heavy wooden stick. The violence made people lose hope for the future and want to end their lives.

If we say a real war like in Iraq or Ukraine is a cruel killing machine, the Cultural Revolution was the same but in a soft way. You never knew when that "bomb" would hit your family. Everyday life was dangerous in a landmine zone.

After months of violence from the Red Guard movement, I felt numb to hear of people losing their lives. It happened in every neighborhood. At twelve, I felt nothing could put a smile on my face. I hated what I had seen.

How could the world have changed overnight? I refused to believe it, but the black ink words were clearly written on large white hanging paper posted on our front door. What should I say if my friends asked me?

My parents became quiet. They did not laugh and talk to anyone as they used to. I saw the sadness in their eyes, and it pained me. I did not want to bother them more with my unanswerable questions.

The schools were all closed. Besides, the Red Guards determined that all teachers were bad people, so the teachers couldn't speak their minds anymore. I had lots of questions but no answers. Hiding at home every day, I did not want to talk to anyone.

Realizing that I could never again be a good student as I always had been was a weird feeling, and it hurt. I did not know how to adjust to this new reality as a child.

The Red Guards classified people into different categories. The entrepreneur belonged to the group "Bad Six." Number one was landlords who owned extensive lands for farming; #2, wealthy farmers; #3, anti-revolutionaries; #4, bad elements; and #5, right-wing conservatives. There were no specifications for every definition. My father was in the last category, #6: capitalist (资本家). There were no traditional laws anymore—whatever the Red Guards said was law, and it changed constantly. I learned to be low-key and hide away from the public eye. I saw the limits in my future adult life: a bad blood child would never get into college or have a good job. I could not understand why all this had to happen to me.

After a few weeks passed by, I went out of my house one day and looked around in the *long-tang*. One of my friends in the neighborhood saw me. She immediately ran toward me and was so happy. I still remember her big smile to this day. She took my hand and asked, "Hey, how are you? Why have I not seen you for a long time?"

I looked at the end of the *long-tang* with a sense of unease, not having a proper answer. "I am OK," I replied.

"I missed you. Come out again tomorrow, OK? We will find something to do."

I nodded and felt a warm stream passing through my heart. I smiled back at her. For the first time in a month, I found that friendship was precious. We played jump rope until my mother called me for dinner again and again. I was sweating and laughing so hard with her. I could not describe how special and overwhelming the happiness was in my soul that afternoon. It meant so much to me at that lonely time. For a while, I could forget how much had changed. It showed me that as long as my friends still played with me, as long as my mother still put food on our dinner table every day, and as long as the sun still rose in the morning, I was not alone. That afternoon added something to my heart that I could never forget.

Some of my friends in the *long-tang* had a lot of sympathy for me. Their parents complained about the Red Guards calling me out that night. Why should they do it to a child? But people only could say it in private. Complaining about the Red Guards was a crime, so this kind of conversation was carried out at home behind closed doors.

After that night's raid, our two bedrooms were sealed with boxes and furniture inside. The Red Guards took all our bank accounts but could not find the hidden gold they expected. They ordered my parents and me to sleep in our living room.

Now we used it as a bedroom, living room and dining room. The black piano was sealed by white paper sealers, so no one could play.

My aunt and uncle used to dine here every day but now decided to carry their meals to their third-floor apartment, trying not to make my parents and grandmother feel cramped.

September came, and all the schools were still closed. I stayed home like everyone else, hanging out with other kids all day in the *long-tang*. We wasted much time playing games and wandering around doing nothing for more than a year.

My mother's school was closed. She now worked nearby, washing medicine bottles in return for a small salary. My father's salary of 190 yuan shrank to 48. My mother would do any work to make even a little money to help the family financially. Dad was ordered to an eyeglass factory. He was already over sixty years old, and the hard labor took a toll on him, but he never complained. After the June raid, he lost all his management titles at work, but he did not talk about it. However, I saw him sitting in the chair, staring at the floor for a long time. With me around, he was always calm. If I asked him why he was unhappy, he would say, "You are too young to understand." I was not happy with that kind of answer.

When I was growing up during these years, I gradually learned that being Chinese, you had no choice but to obey. Speaking your mind was a very dangerous thing.

The physical labor made Dad come home tired. His hearing worsened quickly from the loud factory machines. Sometimes I had to yell when talking to him. However, my father was an optimistic person. Even in such a difficult time, he was always cracking jokes. At dinner time, what made him a happy man was a glass of Chinese wine. It was supposed to be served warm, so he put a small wine cup inside a larger bowl of hot water to heat the wine to the perfect temperature. I sat next to him and enjoyed the smell of the sweet fragrance when he sipped it. When Dad was home, our house was alive. He brought laughter back.

Food supplies were still low at the beginning of 1968. One day my mom came home and told me that she had sold her wedding ring to buy food for the family. I felt so sad to look at her finger, with its deep trace from her white gold wedding ring.

As a family, we shared dishes at our dinner table. Grandmother often put my favorite food on my plate. My father would say, "Mom, you should enjoy it yourself. The kid will have opportunities to have more when she grows up," but Grandmother still pushed the meat dishes toward me as if she hadn't heard him. During family mealtimes, I learned to always consider others before treating myself and always share the best things. I often acted as a copycat, pushing Grandmother's dishes back to her again. She would smile and say, "You are silly, playing chess with me again."

Thinking of others and sharing food with loved ones were always essential traits. I learned them not only from the adults' instruction but also from the examples they set. My mother used to say, "When we share good things with loved ones, we double the happiness. If we share sadness, we will get half of it." It was so true, especially in difficult times. We were not rich, but we were happy every day.

The Red Guards took my father's beloved Leica camera but left the large stereo system. Every evening, when Grandmother finished her housecleaning, the thing she most loved to do was listen to *Ping Tang* (评弹), a form of southern Chinese opera with a beautiful soft melody. Grandmother's hearing was weak, so she often put her head next to the radio speaker while sitting on the sofa with her eyes closed. Many times, I thought she had fallen asleep, but Grandmother never did with her favorite songs. As I played around the house, I listened to the lovely lyrics repeated over and over again. I learned the lovely melody and a lot of classic Chinese stories from my grandmother's radio programs. We went from rich to poor, but our house was still filled with music and laughter.

Six months after the Red Guards sealed our bedrooms, they came back to take everything left in the rooms: boxes of documents, the whole set of our bedroom furniture, my mother's and grandmother's jewels, fur coats, etc.

My father liked to keep good records for work. The Red Guards used this to accuse him of scheming to get the country back to old capitalism. When they left, they gave my father a useless receipt that listed all the family belongings they had taken. Many years later, we received 300 Chinese yuan from them for everything. It was a true robbery! But nobody dared to call it that.

Not long after the Red Guards took away our belongings, a representative from the housing department (房管处) came, demanding that we give up the whole second floor. My parents had no choice but to obey.

After two weeks, two families moved in. The old kitchen was put back to its original function and shared by four families: my uncle, us, and the two new families. My grandmother slept in the small room that used to be the temporary kitchen. In her original bedroom now lived a couple with a boy. Another couple with two kids moved into our bedroom. We were all squeezed together with no privacy.

Grandmother was in her mid-eighties and well-regarded by our neighbors. One day I overheard a neighbor asking my mother if Grandmother had survived the raid OK. Neighbors were worried that she would commit suicide. As a widow, my grandmother lost her husband when she was twenty-seven years old and never remarried. She raised three boys alone. Now the Red Guards had taken all her life savings and precious jewelry—how could she live with her life?

To everybody's surprise, Grandmother was calm as usual. She still got up early every morning, swept the courtyard quietly, took care of her flowers, and cooked breakfast for the family every morning. Being strong was the only choice. Grandmother was the magical fairy who brought love and held our family together.

Sometimes, her philosophy hit me hard, and I could not agree. In the spring, Grandmother would buy some baby chickens. We had a beautiful wooden cage built by Lao Si for these fluffy little balls. Grandmother gave me the job of feeding them every day with vegetables and rice.

As soon as I opened the cage door, my little confused cuties would jump to my rice regardless of who should be next. Compared with vegetables, rice was a treat for the chickens. I loved watching them fight for food after I picked up the warm eggs from their mom, the hen. Hunting for food must be the nature of any life: animal or human.

The hardest time for me was when my grandmother decided to cook chicken for dinner. I never had the heart to witness the killing process. They were my babies! Even my dad could not watch the murder. I usually hid in my bedroom to avoid hearing the sound of killing.

However, Grandma said that was the way it was. The chicken was raised for humans to consume. She was a farmer's daughter; strong and realistic was the way she had been brought up. At the dinner table, we all enjoyed the young birds. The dish was so delicious, nobody remembered the sad story in the kitchen earlier that day.

Grandmother had fair skin and always dressed in a clean-cut, classic black outfit, with her gray hair neatly combed into a bun. I often saw her mixing the Asian elm tree wood shaving （刨花） with water to make a special hair conditioner. It was popular among middle- and upper-class ladies in Shanghai then. She put one piece of the long, thin wood shaving into a bowl of cold water. Overnight, the water would become sticky later, and in the morning, Grandmother would put the liquid into her hair to help style it neatly. Finally, she put a beautiful hairpin made of ox horn on top of the bun. In my eyes, Grandmother was beautiful and elegant. She was like an oil painting hanging in a museum, ageless.

We were not allowed to hire domestic helpers anymore. The Red Guards ordered my parents to do everything themselves to be "educated" and live at the same level as workers and peasants.

Six months after the raid, things were quietening down. The Red Guards left us alone. One day Grandmother brought home a middle-aged woman with a big smile. She lived nearby and would spend a few hours a day at our house helping with household work.

We called her Sister Chan because Miss, Mrs., and Ms. were prohibited from being used at that time. The Red Guards declared those titles were bourgeois. Sister Chan was a happy woman who always had a warm smile. Her son was one of my playmates in the *long-tang*. She worked for us for many years as a cleaner. I guess Grandmother liked her very much. Mom had to work at the bottle-washing place during the day, and Grandma was getting older and finding housework tiring. She missed the time when she had domestic helpers.

After the Red Guards squeezed us into a small living space, I often heard Grandmother talking about the big house she used to own in another part of Shanghai. She lived there with her three sons until the Japan–China War started. The Japanese air force rained firepower on Shanghai with their air bombers. The bombing turned Grandmother's house and the

My family. From left to right: I, my grandmother, my dad, and my mom in 1965.

neighborhood into ashes. Everything was burned down to the ground. Luckily, the family had left earlier, so no one was hurt. But most belongings were destroyed in the fire and then vanished with the wind.

Every time Grandmother talked about the big house, her eyes turned bright, and her face lit up. I could imagine the rich life she enjoyed in the big house and her most profound regret for having lost it during the war.

As I heard the adults repeatedly describe it, the house was typical of the classic Shanghai courtyard dwellings with two floors and two wings: the main section of the building faced south, with maximal sunlight in the winter but minimal in the summer to keep it cooler.

The house also had west and east wings. It was about three times larger than the house we were currently living in. I never knew what the big house looked like, because no picture of it existed (it was before cameras and photographs were common). All the memories were in my grandmother's head after everything was burned away by the fire.

Grandmother obviously missed her good old life. A part of it disappeared with the Japanese war; another part was gone with the Communist takeover; and the last pieces were taken away during the Cultural Revolution.

I often think Grandmother was a perfect example of a strong Chinese woman. No matter what tragedies struck her, she always remained the family's leader. When everything went wrong or was destroyed, Grandmother picked up the leftovers and went on with her family. "Never giving up" was in the spirit of her bones. She still was the rock of our family.

CHAPTER 10

BACK TO SCHOOL

After almost two years, the government decided to re-open elementary and high schools nationwide. I was in fifth grade when my school closed. Now, all of a sudden, I was in high school.

Colleges remained closed. A generation of Chinese youths had no college for over ten years. If you happened to grow up in these years, that was the life you must face. Homeschooling was not legal.

If taking away a child's right to learning is a crime, then taking away a generation of children's rights to education was one of the biggest crimes in modern history.

Since the first grade, my class had always had fifty kids as a standard size. Students were supposed to manage their studies to fit the teacher's style so that teachers could concentrate on managing their time by explaining all the requirements and materials.

Sometimes the teacher was a fast speaker and I would need more time to understand the text. I had to take notes as fast as possible, then go home to re-study and digest the text at my own pace. We were not allowed to interrupt the teacher with questions in class because they always had a plan for the full forty-five minutes.

Moving to the U.S., I discovered that parents constantly complained classes were too big. My daughter's elementary school class had fewer than fourteen kids. The only explanation I could think of was that the school had enough resources. How lucky Americans are.

When the K12 schools reopened, I found my new classroom similar to the old one back in 1966. The only change was that every morning before the regular class started, we had a half-hour session of reading Mao's quotations from the *Little Red Book*, a collection of the 267 quotes considered the most important wisdom of the Communist chairman.

It was such a dull start to the day! I quickly memorized most of the book. Its omnipresence ensured that only ideas consistent with Mao's quotes were deemed acceptable. In later years, some people compared it to the religious service at church, but it contained very different concepts and ideologies. The *Little Red Book* was a bible to 700 million Chinese in the mid-1960s to late 1970s. It was very powerful for the cult of Mao.

There was a new standard decoration in each classroom: a picture of Mao, dressed in his famous suit, in the center above the blackboard and his quotations printed neatly on both sides of the wall. Each classroom was assigned to two teachers. They were in charge of our attendance, behavior, and, most important, our thoughts.

One of my teachers was a young man with a distinguished Sichuan accent, a Communist Party member who had just graduated from college. We nicknamed him "Little Sichuan". He was an easygoing but stiff guy.

In general, Chinese teachers were authority figures with a Buddha's face. They did not share jokes with kids or act like their buddies. During the Cultural Revolution, Mao encouraged the student Red Guards to attack their teachers, and student–teacher relationships grew tense. Most teachers got humiliated or even beaten by their students, but the job of being a teacher was still an honorable and respected one. Teachers were always highly regarded by parents, thanks to the solid block of Chinese culture that respected intellectuals. It was evidence of the powerful influence of Confucianism on daily life. No students were supposed to challenge their teachers in the classroom. However, Little Sichuan was an exception. He let us treat him like a friend. We were never afraid of him.

I also had a Chinese literature teacher, Ms. Deng, as our deputy teacher. Little Sichuan respected her a great deal. She was a tall, skinny woman in her late fifties, wearing a pair of thin, golden-framed glasses that drew attention to her huge, deep eyes, big nose, and white skin. When she came to my house to check on our small group's progress, my grandmother gave her a nickname behind her back: *the foreigner teacher.* I wondered if she had Western blood, but I never asked.

Ms. Deng was one of the finest literature teachers I have ever had. She could make a boring classic Chinese literature class enjoyable. I sat in the second row in the center of the classroom. Ms. Deng always liked to look at me when she talked to us.

When I was bored, I would take a piece of paper and start sketching her face. Her thin hair, high cheekbones, long face, and large shining eyes behind those glasses were easy to catch on paper. She thought I was taking notes and even talked to me more when she saw me scribbling away.

On one of the parents' evenings, my mother did not have the time to attend. Auntie volunteered to go, but she was hesitant initially because she'd never met Ms. Deng, the hostess for my class.

I immediately jumped up to help: "Don't worry, Auntie. I will draw a picture of her for you. It is easy."

Auntie did not take me seriously or pay attention to what I said. Two minutes later, I handed her my quick pencil sketch.

"Hahaha, she is a ghost!" Auntie could not help laughing, her eyes wide open.

"Yeah, Ms. Deng is just like that." I nodded with complete confidence. I had drawn her hundreds of times and had become very skillful.

When the parents' meeting was over, Auntie returned home. She laughed as she stepped into the house: "I have met your teacher, Ms. Deng. She looked exactly like the cartoon you drew! Hahaha, I recognized her at the first glimpse."

Teachers usually cannot remember every one of their students, but every student would have one favorite teacher in their mind forever. Ms. Deng was that teacher to me. Many years later, when I took my national college exams, one of the sections in the Chinese literature exam that was worth a significant number of marks was translating a classic Chinese paragraph into modern Chinese. The article did not have any punctuation. It was extremely tough to guess the meanings of the ancient writer. All the methods I applied to solve it were things I had learned in Ms. Deng's class. It worked perfectly.

When the schools just reopened, the government's education department started a so-called "Education Reform." No one knew what that meant.

The authorities first changed three years of middle school and three years of high school to four years (zhongxue中学) combined and changed elementary schools from six years to five. Then they tried to speed up the teaching pace for the curriculum. Back then, Chinese schools and businesses had a six-day working week.

However, learning was a process that took time, effort, and absorption. Regardless of how the government pushed, students were still behind the curriculum schedule at the end of the school year. In the meantime, the government education department started a "Re-education" program. They believed that city kids were naïve and spoiled by a comfortable life. They wanted us to work shoulder to shoulder with factory workers and peasants to learn how complex and challenging life could be so that we could grow up to be vital for the country. Classroom education, which in the past had always been emphasized, now became less important.

To undermine education, which was so central to people's hearts, overturned thousands of years of Confucian principles. Mao was a rebel against his own heritage. People did not know whether it was a good reform or a bad screw-up for the country. They were confused but vividly remembered the brutal turbulence of the recent past. The violence of the Cultural Revolution kept most people silent about their political thoughts. People were scared. They would rather obey and be at peace than take the risk of speaking out.

When I was seventeen, I met my first boyfriend in high school, and my whole family was on high alert. Dating in schools was prohibited.

He was the son of one of my mother's colleagues. They both taught in the same school. The boy was good at all subjects at school. We discussed homework. His views on some topics opened my eyes to the world. I appreciated and shared some homework subjects with him, especially in culture and arts. We helped each other and had a lot in common as well. I never paid attention to the romantic side of the friendship.

When he visited me, I saw my aunt talk with him with a big smile. I believed my whole family liked him as a good boy. Auntie and Uncle especially enjoyed chatting with him, but as a teacher, Auntie was very aware that dating was forbidden for teenagers. Every day, I tasted the freedom that my family gave me and felt the massive pressure in school.

At that time in Shanghai, the Cultural Revolution was close to the end, but the society was not back to normal. People did not have a clear idea of what was right or wrong.

As a group, young women were not well respected, which made them vulnerable. When people gossiped, they always intended to criticize the female in the scenario. Auntie knew it all too well. Both before and after the Revolution, an honorable young woman's name was always very important in society. Auntie tried to protect me. How? The best way—the only way—was to prohibit any romantic relationship from happening. I felt the pressure creeping in.

I still talked to him at school, but we never became close friends again. We could not discuss our favorite subjects anymore. I constantly sensed there were so many eyes watching me. Even with my rebellious spirit inside me, I was afraid. The culture was powerful; I knew I would never win against it. 'Obey' was the big word in the sky. So, eventually I stopped talking to him altogether and felt terrible about the whole thing for a long time.

Summer was coming. My class got a new assignment: to work at a cotton textile factory in Shanghai to "learn from the workers."

It was June. The hottest, most stifling time in Shanghai. The factory workers had three shifts. Every shift was eight hours, including a half-hour meal break. The shift pattern rotated every week, making me feel constantly tired, as if I never had enough rest.

The textile workshops were huge, hot and very loud, with hundreds of high-speed machines running all day and night. Of course, in 1970, there was no air conditioning. I was about sixteen years old. The workload was the same as for the adult workers. My role was watching and keeping a machine running. My excitement and curiosity about the new job disappeared quickly in the noise of the workshops. By the end of my eight-hour shift, I was exhausted. During work, the tiny cotton pieces flew from the textile machinery to my nose. Some were stuck in my sweating skin. It made my face and body constantly itchy. As soon as the clock pointed to the end of the eighth hour, I ran to the shower room as quickly as possible.

The first day I entered the vast facility, I was stunned. It was a big room without separating walls. Everyone could see everyone naked! Even if it was single-sex only, it was still unbearable and embarrassing for me as a teenage girl. But I did not have another choice and tried. Closing my eyes and let the water fall on my body, I washed as fast as possible.

I got used to the weird environment after a long time and survived. Every day at the end of work, the warm water massaged my tiredness muscles and took the itching cotton away from me. The water and soap made me a new person again. Then I would jump on my bike and fly home.

In the factory, it seemed no one cared about employment protections for untrained teenagers like us. These kinds of working conditions were standard in a modern city in 1971. One of the girls in my class got her arm seriously injured because she was not strong enough to stop the fast-running machinery of the textile mill. I quickly learned how to manage safety and protect myself. I had to. The factory workers were kind, treating us like their own children. But I had learned nothing about the class struggle.

CHAPTER 11

THE COUNTRY GIRL

After four months of working my tail off in the textile factory, my class was sent to a village on the outskirts of Shanghai to "learn from the peasants." This time, I lived there for another four months.

On a cold March morning, I said goodbye to my parents, uncle, auntie, and grandmother. A bus shipped us to a village in suburban Shanghai. I was not scared to go because a lot of neighborhood kids were sent there and returned home.

The spring sun was solid and warm. Getting off the bus, we hiked for an hour to reach the assigned address. This was the first time I walked on a small ridge not paved by asphalt or stone.

Soybeans were planted around the roadsides to save room in the field for crops. Every inch of the farm soil was treasure for the peasants. Hundreds of little purple-white soy flower were waving in the wind as a welcome sign to us.

The hiking was filled with adventures for a city girl like me. This was a typical southern Yangtze River area—a peaceful water country. Streams and rivers made an endless network for the landscape. The village was located in a flat field with a mountain in the distance and a river around its edge. We had to cross many narrow, one-piece wooden plank bridges without handrails.

In the afternoon, we hit the first single-plank crossing. It was about one foot wide and twenty feet long. It had no handle we could hold onto for balance. The fast-running current flowed just a few feet underneath. None of us dare to walk onto it. When I stepped on it, it swung ominously.

One girl suggested that we hold each other's hands. Good idea! It is incredible how hand-holding could help us psychologically, even though I know we would still all fall into the river if one of us did. Hand in hand, we moved inch by inch in a single line.

Finally, we passed it! In this snail-like way, we carefully crossed the narrow plank bridges and eventually reached our destination before dark.

A month later, all of us could run over any of the bridges like the local kids, even on a slippery rainy day with mud on our shoes. Maybe this was part of what they called "learning from the peasants."

To house us for the four months of our stay, the school rented rooms from the village residents. I stayed in a large bedroom with seven girls. Each of us brought a simple wooden bed from home, shipped here by the school.

There was no indoor plumbing, no shower. We used a wooden pot as a toilet like the villagers did every day. Every morning, taking turns, two of the girls would empty the pot into the septic tank, then wash it in the river. We had never done this at home, and I hated this disgusting job, but it was a duty and part of the peasants' daily life, which we were required to experience.

The septic tank was located just outside our toilet room window. Every day, we had to move the heavy pot across the house's zigzag hallway, then go through the back door, passing the vegetable fields to the septic tank. One girl moved forward while the other moved backward. It was a difficult journey.

One day, I invented a shortcut. I had my coworker lift the pot higher and pass through the window in our toilet room with me so we could get it to the septic tank in less than half the distance.

Before I had the chance to celebrate my "smart" idea, I heard our landlady yelling and complaining to Little Sichuan, who was staying with us in the village: "Go tell your girls they cannot do it! Moving a toilet over a window is bad luck for my family. Don't you understand? The kitchen gods will get angry!"

Really? I felt a sense of guilt while Little Sichuan kept apologizing to her. My innovation was killed in the cradle.

The river that ran through the village was the only water source. People used it to irrigate fields, wash vegetables, and wash the toilet as well. The tide flowed in the direction of the water. The same water came back later in the day in the other direction. One day I saw a small dead pig floating on the river to the left of our house. On the same evening, it came back in the opposite direction! Life in the village was like water in the river in the way it came and went, day to day, year to year. It had never changed in a thousand years.

To prepare drinking water, the villagers used alum, a chemical that one could buy from the grocery store, to separate dirt from clean water, discard the heavier dirty part in the bottom of the water and use the clean part for cooking and drinking.

All water must be boiled to drink. We followed the villagers' example in every element of our daily lives and were totally re-educated by the end of the fourth month there.

Every morning, we met the boys staying in a nearby villager's house. Under teacher Little Sichuan's supervision, we gathered in the kitchen for breakfast, which was usually heavenly rice porridge. It was better than sushi rice because it was freshly cut, rich in moisture, soft, and pungent. Breakfast was always followed by mandatory "Morning Study," reading the quotations from Mao's *Little Red Book*.

Our budget for food was tight. The money came from school and our parents. The meals were simple—mainly rice and bok choy—but they were very fresh, going straight from the farm to the table.

We never ate seafood. It must have been too expensive. Luckily, two boys on our team knew how to cook. They both were from working families with siblings. Lacking parenting care during the day had made them very skillful in housework. Little Sichuan immediately put them in charge of the kitchen.

At the age of seventeen, we were always hungry. Everything tasted good at dinner time, even without meat or seafood. When night came, the girls were having a sleepover party every night. We would gossip, tell jokes, and laugh endlessly, each lying on our individual bed, covered with a white mosquito net. It was like a small private room. Mosquitoes were everywhere with their unique humming sound, ready to bite at any minute. In summer, it was impossible to sleep without the net tightly above the bed.

Every night we made lots of noise, laughed, and talked in our room, but our landlady never complained. One day, I met her in the hallway, she looked at me with a smile, said, "Hey, girl, do you know you are at the happiest age of your life? Enjoy it." She must have envied and loved us. I did not understand what she meant back then. We were complaining about our problems all the time.

Life in the suburban village was simple and boring. There was not a single store. If I wanted to get snacks, I had to hike to the nearby town center, which was miles away. It was a new experience I would never have had as a city kid.

The good days did not last long. The weather got warmer very soon. The busy growing season arrived.

Located south of the Yangtze River plainland, Shanghai was hot in summer and rich in rain. The unique weather made this area an excellent region for growing rice, the most important crop in China.

However, growing rice requires much hard work. People often said rice fields were so beautiful in photos, especially when viewed from the terraces. The green hills were stunning. But when I look at these pictures today, the very first thing I see is the tremendous workload for the peasants. During growing seasons, rice fields require about foot-high water. In the summer, the areas were like a vast, hot mirror reflecting the burning sun without mercy.

While working under the sun, I felt like a sandwich getting baked: the sun was grilling me above, and the water was steaming me from the bottom. We were cooked well every day. Besides that, there were all kinds of insects trying to bite me. In the evening, the mosquitoes were all out, like little helicopters mercilessly hungry for our blood. I told myself I would never want to live here, no matter what.

My grandmother was from a farmer's family, growing up in the fields, who used to say, "Every grain of rice needs seven *dan* (担) water to grow." A *dan* was a tool to carry water on people's shoulders in the countryside in old times: a long bamboo pole with two large buckets of water on each end. One *dan* carried more than ten gallons of water.

From an early age, I was not allowed to drop rice on the table and discard it. Grandmother called it a "sin." She taught me that rice needed so much work, from planting to harvesting, that we must not waste it.

The village people prepared the rice fields for the season themselves and did not bother to use us as free labor. The work required skill. If the crops did not grow as planned, the whole season would be wasted, and they could be starved. However, they did not let us be lazy either.

We were assigned to apply fertilizers in the rice fields. Pig and human waste were the most widely used fertilizers then because they were always available and cheap. Most peasants could not afford chemical fertilizers or pesticides.

Animal manure had a horrible smell. Sometimes it had parasites. The peasants collected it from their animals and allowed it to be composted in a mixture of grass chips for weeks before applying it in the fields.

One day, we were given the job of manuring the rice fields. There were no tools for it. We were told to use our hands to spread it into the wet soil evenly. Also, we had to be barefoot to do it because the field was flooded with half-foot-deep water. I was horrified when I learned about this job! Although I had my rubber rainboots in my room, I was not supposed to use them because the peasants could not afford them. We had come for re-education, so we must be the same as them.

It felt like it would take me forever to get used to the strange feeling of walking on little stones or wet mud barefoot. The sun was baking, and the rice fields were endless. I had no choice. I tried barefoot one day, two days… until the tenth day when my feet were numb. They had got used to it. The skin of the soles must have grown thicker. I had passed the test.

The day we were assigned to spread manure in fields by hand, the air stopped moving. The rain was coming.

It was pig-fermented poop, disgustingly warm and wet in my bare hand. I felt my lungs could not pull in enough oxygen. The air pressure was shallow. I closed my eyes throwing it to the enormous square field in different directions.

Once, I lost control, and the manure directly flew into a classmate's neck from my hands and down into his clothes. I felt terrible and did not know what to say. To my surprise, Little Sichuan came and told me that it was a learning process and it was OK. The boy must have seen my horrified expression, he smiled back as a gesture of forgiveness while he tried to get the brown stuff out of his shirt.

Once the spring seeding season was over, we were immediately plunged into the more horrible summer season without any break. At that time, China had a population of 850 million. Cultivatable land was only about 10 % of the total land. Anywhere especially south of the Yangtze River, where the weather was warm and rainfall was plenty, the rice fields were gold for the poor peasants. They often planted two or three seasons of crops during the warm months. This was known as the Double Rushes (rush to harvest and rush to reseed in a few weeks) in July. They had to gather the spring crops and reseed the fields for autumn growth in one to two weeks. It was extremely tough, grueling work under the scorching summer sun. We got up before sunrise. It was the hardest thing for me to wake up in the morning. So many times, I wished I was home in Shanghai. I missed my bed badly.

Everything was done by manual labor. As usual, we were assigned less-skilled jobs like cutting wheat. Sickles were the only tools to cut, but they were not made with high-quality metal and quickly became dull. By lunchtime, all sickles had to be sent to be re-sharpened nearby. As soon as we finished our lunch, we used the re-sharpened sickles to work again.

The sun was intense and hot. Every day we worked in the wheat fields about fourteen hours, including weekends. The hay needles flew everywhere. I tied my shirt collars and sleeve openings closed, but they still found a way to get inside my clothes. Every evening, I would get water from the river to wash myself off. But at night, when I lay in my bed, I felt that the needles from the wheat ears were still all over me. Compared with the local peasants' workload, ours was much less impressive. We never got a chance to communicate with the village kids our own age. I often wondered what kind of life they would have when they grew up. Did they ever know there was a different world outside their rice fields? Did they want to go out to explore?

When the season was over, I could not wait to go home. I missed my family, my bed, and my shower every day. The village people held a farewell party for us. Together we sang, laughed, and enjoyed lots of food. It was a happy time for everyone. At the moment, I temporary forgot what I had suffered. My heart was connected with the village people.

Just like the previous assignment in the factory, "learn from the workers," I had experienced the love and kindness of ordinary people. It was like good food, pure and raw without seasoning. I had learned hard work from the peasants and that a simple life could be happy and enjoyable. But once again I had learned nothing about class struggle.

When I returned to Shanghai, I found my home was so luxurious and cozy. My bed was extra comfortable. Grandmother was super-happy to see me. My mom cooked my favorite chicken dish. Everyone in my family was surprised to see a "black girl" running around the house; my skin was baked into a red-brown color by the southern China sun. No suntan lotion existed then. My long-sleeved shirt and straw hat were my only "skin protection lotion." I was so happy that my life was back to normal. For the first time, I understood what the word *survival* meant. I had survived.

One day, after returning to school, Little Sichuan called me into his office and told me that Red Guards had accepted me to be a member! I guess my hard work in the countryside had made an impression on Little Sichuan, so he recommended and welcomed me. Why should I join? By 1971, the Red Guard movement had passed its peak and was in decline. Nobody cared to join anymore. I did not care either, but I was not supposed to say "no." To obey was part of being Chinese.

Life was a play in those days. We were all actors or actresses in a show. I should now play a "Red Guard" in my current act. I obeyed.

CHAPTER 12

UNCLE

If there was one person who had the most influence on me and whom I admired more than anyone else in the world, it had to be my uncle Wei Tong Liu, my father's youngest brother.

Uncle Wei Tong and his wife, Jinhua Li, lived with us until the end of 1978. It was a popular way to live with an extended family in China. Three generations living under the same roof was considered a good, happy family lifestyle. The older generation watched the grandkids, so the married couples could go to work without worrying.

Uncle and Aunt lived in the same apartment where my older Uncle Wei Zuo and his family used to reside until they left for Taiwan in 1949. The apartment was small but cozy and private. They had a huge bookshelf with sliding glass doors. It was too big to fit in their room, so they let it sit in the corner of the staircase. The cramped space did not bother them too much. They seemed happy to live with us, sharing the house with my grandmother and my parents.

When the night approached, after I had finished my homework and dinner, the most enjoyable moment for me was climbing the stairs to the third floor and spending some quality time with them. Together they brought Western culture and free thinking into my very young mind from day-to-day life without my realizing it, from which I have benefited my whole life forever.

Uncle was a brilliant scholar with a unique personality, which sometimes could be difficult for others. According to my mother, I was the only one in the family with whom he never got upset. No matter what I said or how I behaved, Uncle never raised his voice at me.

When he went to work in the morning, he always wore a navy blue cap, whether the weather was cold or warm. If it was raining, his cap would function as his umbrella. He never carried an umbrella or a watch. He always said, "Why do I need a watch when clocks are everywhere?" It was true.

Uncle had a broad forehead, and his eyes were penetrating, like a sword to your soul. He had an infectious smile, and his eyes, which curved like the new moon, made you want to approach him. Uncle and Aunt did not have children. They loved me as their own and spoiled me occasionally, but more importantly, they taught me what was good and what was bad. I learned forgiveness and unconditional love from their examples.

Uncle and Aunt were college classmates. He was in medical school, and she was in nursing. Upon graduation, Aunt was sent to Columbia University's nursing education master's program with funding from the World Health Organization. She returned to Shanghai to reunite with her husband in 1949, working as the head nurse of the Women's and Children's Hospital of China in Shanghai. They gave up the possibility of a much better life in the U.S. and returned to Shanghai before the People's Republic of China was born.

One reason for the decision was to be with family, and the other was to serve their country—the new China. At that time, many overseas scholars returned to China. The old Chinese party of government (Kuomintang also referred to as the Chinese Nationalist Party) was corrupted, and people were tired of years of wars. They believed that Mao and his new government would finally improve China. They wanted to be part of it. My uncle was one of them.

After the political powers changed in 1949, the new government ranked all scientists as one of their key strategies to keep top intelligence in Communist China. The young country needed their help to rebuild the economy. As a first-class research scientist, Uncle had the privilege of enjoying many benefits ordinary Chinese people could not dream of, especially during the Great Leap Forward and the Great Chinese Famine, when many were starving to death. He could have a lovely apartment with a private entrance for housing, which he turned down; he was eligible to dine in exclusive clubs, which he turned down; and he was offered extra food coupons for meat, seafood, and other goods, but he turned all of them down. People often asked him why. Uncle would smile and say that he wanted to be treated the same as ordinary people.

Growing up under one roof, I regularly saw my uncle's company's financial manager come to our house to deliver his salary. People were paid in cash bills monthly at that time, and everyone knew everyone else's salary. Uncle received the highest among his colleagues, which made him very uncomfortable. He did not like it and refused to accept it. I often heard the lady to persuade him to take his salary. They would push back and forth with the money.

Uncle only agreed to accept half of his salary. This action gave his finance office a good headache. What would they do with the extra money? After years of struggles, the financial department gave up on him. They decided to put the money into a separate account. Uncle never touched it until 1972. I do not know what made him change his mind, but we were all happy to see him eventually accept what he deserved. However, Uncle never took advantage of his right as a high-ranking research scholar to access other special benefits. Uncle and Aunt still lived like ordinary people in the small apartment on our house's third floor after the Revolution was ended.

Uncle was the most intelligent man I have ever met. He was always the very top student in all his schools. When his older brother Wei Zuo graduated from high school two years ahead of him, Uncle Wei Tong at the age of fifteen stole his older brother's high school diploma, took the national college entrance exam, hit very high scores, and was admitted to Yenching (燕京大学) University. Since the college exam, Uncle Wei Tong switched his legal name with his brother permanently.

Yenching University was one of the most selective colleges in China then. It was a Christian-supported university that changed its name to Peking University after the Communist government took over to prevent the "U.S. empire influences."

Uncle met Aunt in medical school. I loved to hear him tell the funny story of his first date. In late March, he sent a love note inviting Aunt on a date a few days later. She received it and thought it must be a joke, so she tossed it out. Uncle nervously waited at the chosen place on a cold spring night for two hours before returning to his dorm sad and disappointed. The next afternoon, they met on campus. He realized it had been April Fool's Day!

Even after skipping two years of high school, Uncle was always one of the top students in all his classes, among strong competition as he attended one of the best medical schools in China. However, he advised me not to skip any grades as he had because it was a great deal of work for him to catch up. After graduating from Yenching, Uncle and Aunt both attended the Peking Union Medical College (协和医学院).

Uncle had an amazing memory. He could easily read something and memorize it forever without effort, even long Latin medical terms, which he only needed to read once. When I was a kid, I liked to bet on things using memory. Usually, I was always the winner among my buddies; I only lost to Uncle.

There were times when I said, "Let's bet on this question for ten yuan. If I am right, you pay me ten, OK?"

Uncle smiled dismissively. "You have not paid me our last bet of fifty yuan. You can deduct it from there if I lose." We both laughed.

One day during the Cultural Revolution, the Red Guards at Uncle's company called him in, accusing him of being a traitor for publishing his research papers in an English medical magazine outside China. Uncle's main research field was typhus, an infectious disease that was common in the army during the Second World War. Many servicemen died of it due to the unhygienic conditions they faced in wartime. Now it has almost disappeared thanks to improved knowledge and sanitation.

Discussing and exchanging research ideas in international magazines was expected in the science world. However, in the middle of the Revolution, the Red Guards could mercilessly do anything to innocent people. Everyone was afraid of them, but Uncle did not always keep quiet.

He was a firm believer in medicine without boundaries. He argued that if there were no medical research exchange, there would not be today's modern medicine. The Red Guards insisted that they were right.

To everybody's surprise, in front of a large audience, Uncle said calmly, "That was not what Chairman Mao said in his book *Selected Works of Mao Zedong.*" Having memorized the volume and page numbers of the quotations in Mao's books, he told the crowd what Chairman Mao had said about this subject, word for word and accurately.

The Red Guards were stunned and speechless. They were all coworkers of the same publisher, Shanghai Science and Technology Publisher, where Uncle worked as a medical editor until he retired. They knew Dr. Liu's memory was unchallengeable and could not compete with him. The audience members later told Aunt they wanted to clap but did not dare to.

I loved and admired my uncle and aunt as if they were my another set of parents, if not more. With them, I saw how an honest human being with dignity should be; men and women are equal, and girls can achieve the same as boys. If I had a question, my uncle always explained it to me patiently.

Growing up in Chinese culture, I was used to some of my questions being ignored by adults. They would assume that a kid's question was silly and petty. My father sometimes did, but Uncle always took me seriously. And more important was that I felt I was respected as equally as an adult. Sometimes, Uncle did not know the answer to my question for sure. Then he would tell me that he must do some research and return it to me no later than the next day. There was never once he did not give me an answer. He made me feel respected and showed me the highest standard of work ethic that a good scholar stood for.

In most Chinese families, people adjusted how they communicated with others according to their age. The older the person was, the more respect they got. In my family, my grandmother had the most seniority, so everyone deferred to her. Then my parents were the second oldest; and I came last, so I should obey all of them.

Only when I joined a conversation with my uncle or auntie, did I feel totally equal and free to express my thoughts. That was the reason I loved to go upstairs to their apartment every evening.

Because Uncle was a medical doctor, if someone got sick in the family, the first thought was to ask him what to do. One day, my mother got a cold and coughed violently. I was about thirteen years old then and, very concerned, ran upstairs for help. He was reading a book in his armchair.

"Mom is sick and coughed badly last night. What can we do to help?" I asked.

Without lifting his eyes to look at me, he turned his head, pointing to the big bookcase outside the room, and said, "Go and find answers yourself."

Uncle had an extensive collection of medical volumes in his bookcase at the corner of the staircase that led to their small apartment.

I was furious. It was my mother, the most important person in my life, who was sick. How could he be so cold? Suddenly I remembered that in Chinese literature, the word *knowledge* （学问） was made up of two characters: learn and ask. Immediately I hit back: "Knowledge = Learn + Ask. When I do not know something, I ask. It is good that I asked you a question. You should answer me!"

"This saying is wrong," Uncle replied quickly and did not back down. "When I was in college, we went to the library to find answers ourselves."

He said this with a calm tone, looking me in the eye.

I did not know what to say and was still upset. Slowly, I walked toward the bookcase, picked up a medical book and started reading some chapters. He was a medical editor at a publisher then and had a collection of popular medicine books that I could understand. After half an hour, I calmed down and wrote some notes: the names of two medications for a cold and cough. When I showed my "prescription" to Uncle, he smiled and nodded OK.

Running to the drugstore, I got them for my mom. She was well again soon. To this day, I still do not know whether she would have recovered anyway or my picks helped. Maybe it was both.

This was a lesson that I never forgot as I grew up. From that day onwards, whenever I had a question, I always went to the bookcase before asking anyone for help, not even asking my auntie, who was always there for me.

Before I realized it, I had almost read through half of Uncle's books. Later, I found that this home collection was not enough for my growing curiosity toward the world. The library became my primary resource.

Looking back today, I genuinely appreciate what Uncle taught me about the way of learning for a lifetime. In real life, when problems strike, there is often nobody one can ask. Books are silent teachers. The benefits of self-learning are priceless. I hope Uncle can hear me from the sky. He would be smiling.

Uncle was not religious but respected his mother's strict Buddhist faith. We hardly discussed this topic because it was a sensitive issue during that time. When I moved to the U.S. in 1987, I had more opportunity to read the Bible, and I found that what Uncle and Aunt were doing in their daily life in China, very much reflected what the Bible taught.

One favorite thing for Uncle to do in his retirement years was go to the Shanghai Foreign Language Book Store upstairs on the second floor. The bookstore had a remarkable collection of language books. It was only for professionals with permission. Uncle often spent half a day there reading. One day, he came home with a big smile on his face. He had found that his research was quoted in an encyclopedia and a medical school textbook. Uncle was a very cool guy, hardly showing his emotions. But that day, he was so excited, as if he had found something he had been seeking for a lifetime.

After retiring from his publishing job, Uncle wrote a final paper summarizing all his research; his whole life's work. He worked so hard, day and night, concentrating on his ideas that sometimes Aunt was worried he would get sick.

Uncle was so relieved when he finished his final paper. He then sent it to one of his colleagues in the U.S. and asked for it to be circulated among his medical associates but not to be published in English magazines, saying: "I do not want to have any political trouble in my old age, but I just wish to share my work with the medical world…"

Uncle hated wars, especially WWII, which destroyed his career and dream. After Pearl Harbor, all American professors in the medical school were called back to the U.S. and the school closed its Beijing campus. Uncle was very sad about the news, but he could do nothing.

He continued his research in the hospital where he was a resident. As I knew, typhus was a disease spread by ticks. Patients could die if they did not get treatment quickly. In the '40s, there were no medicines to cure typhus. Uncle's work was critical. Every day, he fed the lab ticks with his own blood three times a day. Even without the help of his American medical professors, his work had outstanding results. His published research paper was requested by medical societies all over the world.

Not too long after that, in 1948, Uncle was called to see the American Ambassador, Mr. John Leighton Stuart. Mr. Stuart was also the first president and the founder of their school—Yenching University. Mr. Stuart surprised him with an award he never expected: the award for his outstanding achievement in an extremely difficult environment. Uncle took this as the greatest honor. Before the Sino-Japanese War, he had dreamed of getting Nobel Prize in Medicine, but his hopes perished with the war and then the 1949 Communist takeover of China.

During those years, China was a closed country. Studying English was not a popular choice. Auntie volunteered to give English lessons to our neighbors' kids for free. I often attended her small class in her third-floor apartment.

When people learn a language, they also learn the culture. In an isolated country, Auntie opened the door to the Western world for many young people like me. Later, many of us passed the college entrance exam and graduated.

Sometimes, I heard people ask her why she did that. She said it was passing the time. I knew it was not only to pass the time. She loved children with all her heart. No matter where they came from, poor or rich. Teaching them to be better

*Uncle Wei Tong (second on the right) at the award ceremony
with American Ambassador John Leighton Stuart (First on left)
in the American Embassy in Nanjing, on May 2, 1948.*

human beings was her most enjoyable thing to do in those dark days. She helped people change their lives without expecting anything in return. With kids around, Auntie would laugh so happily. She cared about them very much. I regret that she did not have her own kids, but I feel fortunate to have had her and Uncle as mentors and relatives in my life.

Not too long after their return to China, the Korean War started. Uncle was sent to North Korea as a scientist for bio-chemical weapons research. As soon as he left, his boss at the Academy of Military Medical Sciences (中国人民解放军医学科学院) came to our house, forcing Aunt to give them the U.S. Presidential Award. At that time, no one dared to say "no" to any Party leaders. Aunt gave the medal to the man. A year later, when Uncle returned home from the war, he found out his award was gone and was furious. But he could only express his anger at home when the windows and doors were all closed.

When the Cultural Revolution started, one of Uncle's colleagues took advantage of the free train travel offered as part of what Mao called the Great Networking, designed to spread the words of the revolution, and went to Beijing. When the colleague was touring the Military Museum of the Chinese People's Revolution (中国人民解放军军事博物馆) in Beijing, he saw Uncle's award from the U.S. government was on display. The thing that most shocked and amused Uncle was the exhibit's footnote: "The scientist who won this award voluntarily gave it to the Chinese government and Communist Party to show how much he hates U.S. imperialism and wants to cut off his relationship with them."

CHAPTER 13

TURNING OF LIFE

At the end of 1968, Mao started a new movement called "Up to the Mountains and Down to the Countryside." From 1968 to 1972, millions of youths nationwide were sent from the cities to rural areas. This time it was not like my school assignment. It was a permanent move.

My brother Jian Ping was one of those affected. I never really understood the purpose of this movement. Mao and his government told people it was good to re-educate the spoiled city youths, to make them learn from peasants and real hard life.

The policy began just as Mao and his government were putting an end to the Red Guard movement. The unemployed youth did have a lot of energy. Some formed gangs and got involved in violence. They would have big group fights on the streets of Shanghai, creating huge problems for the government and economy. Sending them to the countryside was a quick solution to get rid of hundreds of thousands of unemployed young people on the city streets.

The high school classes from 1968 to 1969 were called "All-Red." They were 100% sent to rural areas, regardless of their family situation. For the classes of 1966 and 1967, whose graduations had been delayed by the Cultural Revolution, and the classes of 1970 and 1971, the rules were different: it was measured by how many children of the family lived in the city. If the first child lived in Shanghai, the next one would be sent away. Then the same cycle went on and on.

All my other brothers and sisters graduated early and got jobs in cities. Jian Ping could not qualify to stay in Shanghai. He had to pay the price for his sisters and brother. It was a nightmare for so many Chinese parents in these years. It hurt my godmother deeply.

In these unpredictable years, people could not plan for their future; you never knew what news tomorrow would bring. It all depended on the Party and the government's decisions. People would never know what fate would fall on them until that day came. Jian Ping had no idea he would be sent to Anhui, one of the poorest areas in China.

The schools used a black brush pen to write every graduate's name and where they would go on an outstanding red paper, then posted it on the wall on campus. It was a strange and sad way to decide a young person's future, but it was standard procedure at every school in Shanghai then. The red color symbolized happiness and importance in China; the authorities tried to set up a positive tone.

When I asked Jian Ping many years later about his experience in the village in Anhui Province, he took a deep breath and told me that his first year was really tough.

It started snowing on the second day after he arrived in the village. At night, the temperature dropped to sub-zero Celsius. For weeks he and another young man from Shanghai stayed in a room converted from a barn which had no heat. They had to use paper to seal the windows to stop the wind from blowing in. They slept on hay for the softness of a mattress. Some mornings when he woke up, he would find his blanket wet with frost that had formed from his breath overnight.

During the day, Jian Ping and his roommate tended crops in the fields of the commune and fed pigs and chickens. It was hard work, but Jian Ping had a positive attitude and said he tasted freedom without his parents' control.

However, I saw it was much harder on my godmother. She felt heartbroken for her baby. Being a strong woman, my godmother never showed sadness on her face. Every time I went to visit her, she tirelessly talked about her poor boy in the faraway village and how lucky I was because I had been adopted by the Lius and therefore counted as an only child. Under the current policy, I was allowed to stay in Shanghai. My godmother was happily taking credit for deciding to give me away. She wanted me to share her feelings and appreciate her decision. I did not know if I did.

In fact, during the '70s, the difference in quality of life between rural Anhui and Shanghai was night and day. Jian Ping would have starved if his family had not sent him food.

Jian Ping's horrible experience in the country took a toll on my godmother. She worried about him a lot and could not fall asleep. But there was nothing a mother could do. The village had no telephone. The letter was the only way of communicating with Jian Ping. I wrote to him as much as I could to support him, hoping to be a small light during his lonely days.

My class was scheduled to graduate in 1970, but we were delayed a year by the school closures. When I reached my high school graduation, colleges were still closed indefinitely. Every seventeen or eighteen years old in my class was anxiously waiting for the announcement from the school about what would happen to them. The graduates in the years before me had gone to the countryside, and I was almost sure that I must go too. I prepared myself to leave my warm and loving family.

Ever since I was a baby, I had often got acute tonsil infections. Sometimes the fever was so high that it scared my mother half to death. When I was in kindergarten, my pediatrician suggested having the tonsils surgically removed. My mother agreed it would be a good idea, but she wanted me to make my own decision. My uncle explained that the glands had both good and bad functions simultaneously. They worked as guards to protect me from possible unwelcome outside invasion, but because mine were prone to infection, they often made me unwell.

At the age of seventeen, I suddenly saw myself facing the fact of being sent away and living by myself in an area with no access to doctors. I worried that if I got sick, no one would take me to the nearest hospital, which might be dozens of miles away. I decided to have the tonsils removed.

At that time, acupunctural anesthesia was a new, hot thing. The government promoted it; the media wrote articles about it. Even some doctors said it was good anesthesia. I believed the doctors, just as I trusted my uncle. It was local anesthesia, so I would be aware of everything during the surgery but I should recover quicker.

Looking back to the day of the operation, I realize that I was too brave.

Laying on the table, I watched as the nurse put the tiny needles into my body and ears to induce acupunctural anesthesia.

The long metal acupunctural needles, connected to an electronic device, made the acupuncture points feel sore and tingly. No one explained the procedure to me. I did not know what to expect, but I trusted them as professionals. Uncle was not a doctor in this field. He could not give me more advice. After the prep procedure, the doctor told me to open my mouth. Everything went so fast. Afterwards, I did not remember it much, only felt extreme pain, once when the first tonsil was pulled out of my throat, then a second time to the other side. I felt as if the glands tore out. It was so painful. There was no anesthesia at all. I felt as if they had cheated me!

Years later, the Chinese medical society reviewed their guidelines and announced that acupunctural anesthesia only could be secondary to surgery. During the Cultural Revolution, even the doctors did not tell the truth when they were under pressure from the Party authority.

Thank God I recovered quickly without complications and enjoyed eating a lot of ice cream to stop the bleeding.

A few months before I was due to graduate, Little Sichuan exploded into my classroom with unbelievable good news. The government had changed its policy again. This time, some of us would stay in Shanghai. According to the new policy, I got to stay in Shanghai because I was the only child in my family.

So it turned out I did not need to have gone through that surgery and suffered the pain. But no one could correctly plan their future during the Cultural Revolution!

CHAPTER 14

THE MOTOR FACTORY

Despite what we imagine today, working in a factory was one of the best jobs anyone could dream of in that crazy year of 1972.

Colleges were still all closed. Academic excellence was regarded as useless, even silly. But a factory job was lifetime-guaranteed with standard pay and benefits. Plastered on every wall of the streets was the slogan "Learn from Workers, Peasants, and Soldiers." To be a worker conferred an enviably high status in a closed country.

After receiving many congratulations from friends, I started working at a motor factory: a giant place that made direct current motors for ships and trams. I was assigned to the assembling department.

At eighteen years old, I had my first job—a real one, not just for "re-education" anymore. I was excited when I got my uniform. However, the excitement did not last long. The job was easy for me to learn, but the work needed physical strength. At the end of the eight hours, I was exhausted.

In the evenings, the factory offered electrical engineering courses related to its products, and the classes made my life less boring. Even though they did not offer any school credit, I was happy: at least I had some new things to learn.

The first semester of evening school went by quickly. One day, the principal called me into his office. "The school decided to have you give a speech at the employees' meeting next week. Can you prepare it and let me see it first?"

Why me? I did not have anything to say. He explained that the school hoped I would talk about how I performed so well in class.

I did not know how: I was just doing whatever the teacher told us to do. But to say "no" to the principal was unacceptable. So, I told everyone I was an ordinary person like them. If I could do it, they could, too, honestly. The speech went well.

One day, I heard my grandmother tell a neighbor proudly that her granddaughter had spoken in front of more than 1,000 audience members. (In Shanghai, a factory that had more than 1,000 employees was common.) The head of the factory often called entire employees' meetings to pass the Party's new orders periodically.

Within a few years, I went from an apprentice to a skilled assembler, operating different machines. I do not know why, but I never enjoyed being a worker. No matter how much others envied me for the job, I always felt I was an outsider and did not fit in with my coworkers.

The factory offered excellent childcare for free. On the way to work in the morning, I loved watching the new mothers dropping their babies at factory-operated daycare before they arrived. It was such a sweet time for moms and kids to hug goodbye. I saw the exchange of love.

Every day the cafeteria cooked fresh baby food for the daycare. The mothers had two feeding breaks during a working day: a half-hour each in the morning and afternoon when they would breastfeed or nurse their children with freshly cooked food from the factory kitchen. The half-hour feeding period was a great pleasure shared between the mother and the child.

The daycare lady would bring the child from the baby room as soon as the mother entered the facility. Amazingly, they had memorized every baby's face and their mother's. As soon as she received her baby, the mother would hold her precious sweetheart in her arm and rush to another room to feed and play with them. Laughter rang out every minute. All the babies were covered by free health insurance provided by the factory.

The staff benefits were very important to the employees. The daycare service and baby foods were free. I was about nineteen years old and sometimes sneaked out during working hours with a mom to the daycare. She would change her work clothes, wash her hands carefully, then rush to the second-floor heaven of the daycare, for a lovely moment.

There was a clinic on the first floor of this small pink two-story building. The simple medical office had two doctors and one nurse who served the whole staff of the factory. Anyone could see a doctor during working hours, and the doctor would give a sick note if necessary, so the patient was free to go home. If the illness was more serious, the employee would be transferred to a hospital nearby. The clinic also had a small pharmacy for simple prescriptions, shots, and drips.

Compared with what we have in the U.S., this socialist idea was great. It helped the majority of ordinary people who needed medical care. It might not be the best in quality, but it was affordable and free to all. I miss the availability of full health-care. Medicine should not be a privilege.

However, since I left China, the medical and childcare benefits have been cut significantly. It must be the process of learning capitalism.

In the factory, new apprentices were assigned to a mentor who would teach them working skills and everything about factory life. My mentor, Ms. Cia, was a short, energetic woman who always had a smile. I was surprised she could move a heavy motor unit, which I found very challenging. It must have been the years of working that made her stronger. She taught me all the technical skills of an assembler.

Not too long after I got hired, Ms. Cia retired. Women who worked at factories doing physical work were entitled to retire at fifty and men at sixty, both with full benefits and 80% of their salary. However, their wages were very basic and low. It was distributed monthly on a cash-in-hand basis.

As an apprentice, my salary was a standard eighteen Chinese yuan. However, living expenses were very low, with almost no inflation, and that salary would provide a good average living. Life was simple. After a few years, we got a few yuan salary increase, but you never knew when. The government decided. Usually, after three years, an apprentice became a regular qualified worker. At that time, they would get a raise.

Walking through the factory or the city streets, the red color Revolution slogans "Learn from the workers..." were seen everywhere. I never understood what was so good about being a worker, or why they were supposed to be so much better than anyone else? Surely we could learn good things from people from all walks of life. Soon I stopped paying attention to the slogans anymore.

I got along well with the people in my workshop but was never a close friend to anyone. They were kind, straightforward, and easy to be with, but I also felt the distance between us.

I did not have a friend with whom I could chat for hours in the factory. The thought constantly in my head was: How can I leave this tedious job? I wanted to learn new things. More frequently, another question arose in my mind: Why does everyone say this is one of the best jobs? There were times I tried to tell myself to be satisfied with what I had. The more I pushed myself to be OK with it, the more my dissatisfaction grew.

The girls in the workshop had an unofficial gossip "club." They loved to criticize anyone but themselves. The gossip attracted a certain kind of person, drawing them together into a close circle. Unfortunately, I had no interest in it at all and was always out of the loop. It saddened me that I had no heart-to-heart connection with my coworkers, even though I tried very hard.

I was an outsider in a world that I felt I should belong in. Like a kite losing its string in the air, I lost the direction of what kind of person I should be. What was wrong with me?

As a kid, my mother always encouraged me to try new things and learn them for myself. One day, she brought me a pair of hair scissors and asked me if I would like to cut her hair. I was shocked by her suggestion. I had had no training. But my mother smiled and told me she trusted I could do it. That scissor was the only tool I was going to use.

In those days, barbers pushing carts would come to our *long-tang* looking for business. They would come with a toolbox on their cart or bike and cut hair, shave men's beards, and even provide foot care for a smaller charge than hair salons. I started to pay attention to their work when they cut women's hair.

Soon, I got my how-to pictures in my head with reasonable confidence. I started cutting my mother's and aunt's hair very carefully. It seemed my "customers" liked my work. Before long, some of my neighbors made inquiries. I was thrilled and surprised. Thanks to the trust of my first customer, my mother, I became a free hair-cutter.

Somehow, people heard about my skills in my workshop group. One day a woman asked me to do her hair during lunchtime, so I did it up to her expectation. The news traveled faster than I expected. In no time, I became a free haircutter at work too.

My mother used to say that I needed to learn to say no, but I never did. I liked seeing people leave their chairs with a new haircut, smiling.

I was often the busiest girl at lunchtime. Imagine it. My "customers" would run to the cafeteria to get me a hot lunch as a thank-you. Both food and services were free: a fair trade.

When I was in elementary school, my grandmother had a young student of Chinese medicine come to our house every week to perform a massage on her. Amiable and polite, the masseuse always came in the afternoon before our dinner time. Grandma had arthritis in her late seventies and was sometimes in real pain. I would stand by her bed and watch the student work with great interest. I watched closely and tried to copy her.

Later in the summer, my aunt had neck pain. I immediately volunteered: "Auntie, let me try. I know how to massage. It may help you."

Aunt looked at me with doubt, but she agreed to let me try working on her neck. That whole summer, every night after an evening shower, we both went onto the roof deck while the entire neighborhood were in the *long-tang* for the evening cool. I would put my hand on my aunt's neck, starting to roll it over and over, copying the student's methods.

Sometimes, Auntie would scream at my finger's pressure when I accidentally pushed on her acupoints. It could be sensitive and painful, but I knew it was a good sign that I had touched the key points. I even rolled stronger on her. It always worked well. The patient's reaction was important to the therapist. Aunt often asked how my bony little hand could be so strong. I used the bone in the corner of my hand, not pushing but rolling. That was the way I'd learned from the young lady, though she didn't know I was going to copy her.

By the end of the summer, Auntie told me that her neck pain had greatly improved and she felt much less stiffness. I was delighted when she said it.

To my surprise, Auntie said, "I want to thank you for your such good work. Tell me what you want to have, and I will get it for you."

Really? Nobody had ever treated me like that. I told her that I wanted a chestnut cake from a particular bakery. Auntie smiled and said she would go there to get my treat for me.

Usually, I had only ever had a small piece of the cake on someone's birthday. This time, I would have the whole thing all by myself! The cake was rich with buttercream. My stomach was slim and flat during the food shortage years, and now it could not digest rich food properly. There was no way I could eat it all myself, so I donated it to my family. I think it was a lesson that God taught me: sharing good food with people was better than eating it all alone. Looking at everyone enjoying it, I felt that the happiness of sharing was magical. It was worth much more than I had expected.

Back at the factory, a coworker complained of back pain. I thought of the experience of helping my aunt and volunteered to give her a massage. She was not sure if I could do it. With doubt in her eyes, she accepted my offer. "Let's give it a try."

When I finished the massage, she stood up, moved her body, and smiled from her heart. She felt immediately relieved of her pain. She told the others in the shop what magic I had worked on her. The news spread like fire, and before long I was even busier at lunchtime.

I was well-known for haircuts and massages during my seven years there. Many older workers had chronic pain in their backs or joints because of lifelong manual labor; my massage helped them manage their pain. They all said that I had magic hands, and my aunt and my mom said the same thing. Helping others brought me invaluable joy.

I met Yichin when I was an apprentice in this factory, when I was nineteen and he was twenty-four.

At school, I had always been in charge of news publishing. At the factory, I was in charge of editing the workshop wall newspaper. It was written in chalk on a giant blackboard, and I had to write a new issue every two weeks. The system was called "wall newspaper" and was popular in Shanghai at the time because it saved paper and printing expenses in a poor society.

Sometimes I needed an artist's hand to decorate the wall newspaper. Yichin was good at oil painting and chalk drawing. He could use different colors to express the ideas of the articles well. As he was one of my art editors, we worked alongside each other often.

However, all apprentices were prohibited from dating. Like the other young people, Yichin and I tried not to talk to each other during working hours in case someone gossiped.

All young people had their own ways of handling their love. Yichin managed to meet me on my route home. The bike was the most popular vehicle for commuting among younger workers. He would stop in a store along my cycle path. When I passed by, he got on his bike and we would ride together. That was the only time we talked, away from the factory managers' eye.

The authorities claimed that the reason for the no-dating rule was that it would disturb the process of learning to become a good apprentice. I never understood it, but no matter what, we had to cover ourselves and go underground.

I believe that half the apprentices were dating. Love was always in the air, though it might not be visible to the bosses. After I graduated from the three-year training period, our relationship finally became legitimate.

Being a motor factory worker was a distinctive experience that none of my family members ever had. During my seven years there, I learned how the blue-collar class lived. I learned how sweat could change your way of thinking.

CHAPTER 15

THE COLLEGE DREAM

Going to college was an impossible dream for most Chinese youth of my generation. For me, it was more like a fairytale because of my father's background and because my regular classroom education had been interrupted at fifth grade. The college exam was comprehensive and difficult. It was designed for senior high school graduates.

My factory job offered security, a stable income, good benefits, and, best of all: living in Shanghai, the best place in China. People envied me for this. No one expected that I would want to go to college, because when I graduated, I would face the risk to be sent to outside of Shanghai. Shanghai was the heaven of China.

Most of my high school classmates had been sent to the countryside to work as peasants, I was so lucky in comparison. Is there something wrong with me? Why did I not like this job? I told myself to think twice. Then another voice came into my head: "It is not the life you wanted. You have to leave..."

Looking around, all jobs were distributed by the government. As an ordinary citizen, I had no right to choose where to work. It was impossible to change jobs at that time. Going to college was the only way out.

Unexpected things do happen in life. Following Mao's death in 1976, Deng Xiaoping gradually rose to become the Communist Party's leader and along the way started a significant reform: he ordered the reopening of colleges and universities. The national college entry exam was resumed in 1977.

The world suddenly changed again for the people of China, but this time the change was for the better. The government opened the country to foreign investment and permitted entrepreneurs to start businesses.

After Mao's death, the changes in political power meant things happened very quickly; I did not understand the situation, but I saw new opportunities. No matter what, it was a good chance for the country, and maybe it would be good for individuals as well. I was excited watching on the sideline.

In the first year of college reopening, there was a condition for taking the exam: your entry must be approved by your boss—a local Party leader. It could be very tricky. The boss could say "no" without any explanation. There were no laws to protect the individual, and there was no right of appeal.

At that time, job mobility was almost zero. If I got denied by my boss in the factory, it could cost me a future relationship with my possible lifetime employer, a promotion, and even more. As a former business owner, my father was still considered to have "bad blood." I doubted whether any college admissions officer would even look at my application… There were too many negative elements to worry about. I hesitated to send my registration out in the first year and felt sad. The feeling of being a second-class citizen continued haunting me until the following summer.

In the second year, Deng Xiaoping made a significant change: No strings attached. Admissions based on merit. In other words, the employer could not stop an employee from registering for the national college entry exam. After Mao's death, the Party and the government readdressed many issues in the Cultural Revolution, among them the "Bad #6." Deng's party announced that those in category #6 were no longer considered bad people. All of a sudden, my father was resurrected as a good citizen. Entrepreneurship was wonderful again.

This political policy changed tens of thousands of young Chinese students' lives in the summer of 1978. People saw hope in the future. Employers could not stop their employees from taking exams, nor did students' family backgrounds matter. Admission must be based totally on merit. I immediately registered.

But the college exam was extremely hard. How could I make up for all the years of school I had missed, and in such a short time? Where could I find good textbooks? Where should I start? How could I get teachers for so many subjects: geometry, algebra, Chinese literature, geography, history, and English language? How could I have the time to study while I had to work full-time during the day, Monday to Saturday? It sounded impossible, but I still wanted to try.

Deng had a famous quote: "Crossing the river by feeling the stones." It meant that it is better to make steady, step-by-step progress than to take a huge leap. The leaders of the country were looking for directions, too; how could I know what to expect?

However, when a lifetime opportunity struck, one had to grab it fast. Looking at the history of Communist China, it was clear that once the opportunity was gone, it might never come back. The government could change its policy at any time. They were looking for stones to cross the river themselves.

My parents never suggested or discussed whether I should attend college, nor did I ask them. However, there was an agreement in the air: Of course, I should go if I could. At that time, my aunt was an English teacher at a high school. One day she came home with a good news: her school was going to offer review classes to employees' children preparing for college exams! She put my name on the list immediately. I can never thank her enough. That changed my life forever.

The exam was only two months away. I was not prepared. However, as one of the kids who happened to be growing up in this unusual time, I had to make the impossible possible—there was no other choice.

CHAPTER 16

THE IMPOSSIBLE

Every afternoon at 4 o'clock, after eight hours of physical work, I took my shower and jumped on my bike to Auntie's school. The class started at six.

The days were hot and steamy, the summer sun was a fireball, mercilessly baking everything on the earth. I was sweating as soon as I got out of the shower room. In 1978, air conditioning was still a privilege reserved for theatergoers. I brought an old-fashioned paper fan with me. It would be a help in the classroom.

Looking back today, the amount of ground I had to make up seems like an impossible goal, but at twenty-four years old, I was not afraid of the challenges, nor did I understand the concept of failure.

We had three classes with different subjects every evening, Monday to Saturday. The classes really helped me jump from one level to another faster than I could ever imagine. The teachers were all well prepared and gave us a lot of information on how to pass the exam, but I could not memorize all the textbooks in such a short time.

The teachers poured out all their hearts and energy into what they were doing. After ten years of not teaching college prep, they were thrilled to have the opportunity to help us, their own children, and the children of their colleagues, to get through the golden gate of higher education. Forty-five minutes of class time was never enough for each subject. Many times, I just copied the notes from the blackboard as fast as possible and told myself: do not worry, go home and digest them.

The materials covered all the years of middle and high school. I felt as if I was going to drown in an endless ocean. Some topics I had not learned in school because the government had shortened the curriculum as part of the "reform" experiment. As a result, there were a lot of math and science concepts that were new to me. However, there was no one I could complain to. Take the opportunity or leave it? I chose to do it.

In the classes, we often had no time for a question-and-answer session because there was so much to cover to meet the exam requirements. Every student was attempting a mission impossible.

My geography teacher was a man with thin hair but thick glasses in his later fifties. He was a fast talker and had an amazing skill of drawing maps on the blackboard as accurately as they appeared in the textbook.

Concerned that his students needed to learn too much material in such a short time, the teacher tried to analyze what topics would likely be included in the exam so that we would study those parts more intensively. With so many countries on earth, how could he guess correctly?

In the test, the critical subject was Korea. We had not guessed it correctly. I can still recall one of the questions: which side of the Korean Peninsula's coastline is higher than the other?

Suddenly, I remembered what Mr. Geography had taught us in class: If the coastline was smooth on the map, most times, it was the higher mountainside. The messy line was mostly the beach and sand. I answered accordingly.

One week later, Auntie met the teacher on campus. She happily reported to him that I had used his theory and answered the question correctly. He went to heaven!

The teacher trained us not just to memorize but to use analytical skill. It benefited me not only for the test but also for a lifetime. I ought to give all credit to this great instructor.

Every evening at 9:30 pm, classes were dismissed. I jumped on my bike, flying home. After thirty minutes of fast zigzagging, I stopped at the front door of my house. The cycling made my face red and my whole body burn.

After inhaling some dinner my mother had prepared for me, I ran straight to the roof deck to continue studying.

It was July in Shanghai, warm and steamily humid. Thanks to a new housing policy, my uncle and auntie received a new rental apartment and moved out. I happily moved into their small apartment on our third floor.

Inside my room, it still felt like an oven even at 10 pm. The roof deck was paradise for me. I put out a portable light on the pole. My lap was my desk. With cool breezes touching me, I spent two hours revising what had been taught that evening. Because most of the lessons were new to me, I had to teach myself by reviewing my notes again. Then I snuck off to bed so as not to wake up my parents. The next day I would be at the factory workshop again at 7:30 am. This routine was repeated day after day for two months.

My best friend's mother, who lived next door, used to yell at me around midnight from her rooftop: "Go to sleep, baby! Don't study too hard…" I smiled and waved back to her, then continued.

It was a circle of life for that whole summer. I will never forget this difficult but priceless experience. The challenges of learning kept my spirits high and filled me with energy. I absorbed so much new knowledge from two months' review classes and learned what hard work meant, both physically and mentally.

During those two months, there was an endless pile of books to read. It was like an ocean of knowledge to be mastered. With the intensive classes and my daily work schedule, I felt little hope of passing the exam. At one point, I asked myself, "How can I ever be ready for all of this?" But I definitely did not want to stay in the factory for the rest of my life. I was psychologically getting ready for the escape little by little until the date of the examination came round. I kept my peace of mind by keeping going.

My exams occurred on some of the hottest days of the year in a school with no air conditioning. They lasted for three days, morning and afternoon. It was above 32 Celsius in the morning when I arrived.

As the day of the first exam drew closer, I began to develop a low fever. I prayed not to get sick. This was a once in a lifetime opportunity. I couldn't miss it. What could I do?

On the morning of the first exam, I swallowed a fever reduction pill with a big glass of water. Then I managed to wash down a piece of pancake for energy.

Every exam lasted three hours without a break. After an hour and a half, I felt the pill was working on me and had to go to the bathroom. I raised my hand. A woman came and escorted me to the girls' room on the same floor. She waited outside my toilet door with an expressionless face, then led me back to my classroom to continue my test. In the following days, I did not measure my temperature nor dare to take water. I survived it and was so relieved when the three days were over.

A few weeks later, I received the acceptance letter! My mother was sick with cancer and had just had chemo. She'd lost a lot of weight; it was so sad looking at her. I cried in bed every night but pretended I was OK during the daytime. I did not want her to be in pain. Everyone in the family was worried about her. I was especially.

Mom was excited and happy to learn that her little girl achieved something impossible and was going to university. My

I was in college in 1981.

father was an old-fashioned man who did not express his emotions much. The news also made him feel eased from the guilt of making me a "bad blood kid" for the past 11 years during the Revolution. He was proud.

That acceptance letter brought hope back. The hope to regain the education right of a young person. It meant a lot to me and my family. Even my neighbors were grateful to pass this news on to each other.

I could not wait to start my new college life. Quickly, I said goodbye to my coworkers in the workshop. I was excited without even knowing what my new life would be like.

Every morning to the classes, I rode my bike for about forty minutes, flying through the busy, bustling streets in the city center. Often I was riding between buses, like a sandwich ready to get squeezed!

For the first time, I found myself in a class of ninety-five students. In the beginning, I was able to get familiar with only a handful of people who sat near me because of the size of the class. We were not allowed to change seats. As time passed, I became more interested in meeting new people from different backgrounds.

By the end of the first semester, I knew most of them. Some were peasants' sons, the village's first generation of college students. The woman with cute braids sitting in front of me had been raised in Shanghai then sent to the countryside for re-education for five years, but she never gave up learning, always reading alone in her small one-room barn home without air conditioning or heating. She often wished for bad weather so she would be excused from farming. When she talked about her past life, she would be in tears sometimes. Her pain was clear in her eyes.

The guy who sat on my right side was a bus driver, good at math. When I could not solve some calculus problems, I would ask him. He was a good tutor and always happy to help.

I loved my new student life and friends. There was so much to learn from my peers.

It was in the early 1980. People saw hope in their lives now. The mood had changed. They spoke openly about what they thought. The reopening of the universities let ordinary youths feel there was a bright future for them. In school discussions, students could criticize the Party sharply. Even my visiting cousin from California was surprised.

People were visibly happy after the end of the disastrous ten years of the Cultural Revolution. Emerging as the top leader of China after Mao's death, Deng Xiaoping proposed "Four Modernizations" to strengthen Chinese industry, science and technology, agriculture and the military.

Since I had worked at the motor factory for many years, I was qualified to continue receiving my salary when I went to college. Very few students had this benefit as I did. Most of them were from the countryside and did not have paid jobs before entering school.

Looking back today, it was like a dream. College tuition was free in China in that years. With my small salary, I enjoyed traveling to the Yellow Mountain and hiking with friends. It was my first time experiencing life without an adult's supervision.

Mingling with my friends made me realize I was no longer the smartest kid on the block. There were so many classmates who were much brighter than I was, and I had to work my tail off to catch up. Because many students had been denied an education for ten years, everyone was so hungry for learning. Hard work was enjoyable and they wanted to do it.

Because of the school closures, my class of ninety-five people included students fourteen years apart in age. Some students had graduated from high school in the class of '66 and had a solid education. Some had stopped the learning process in middle school. They had some textbook knowledge, then were sent to the country. Some were like me, stopped traditional classes in elementary school and did not get much learning. Some were current-year graduates from high school. They had a solid education too.

The appreciation for education from the older students was stunning. Sometimes, it was hard to pull them away from their desks. After classes were dismissed, they would stay in their seats to continue studying; after my sports practice, they were still there. It was as if they were determined to make up for the ten years they had missed during the Cultural Revolution.

Fortunately, I was not one of the workaholic students. Play and having fun are essential parts of my life. College was the best time of my life. I miss it with all my heart.

From elementary school days to my factory job, I had never been a sports fan. However, my college best friend was my school team's leader, so now I was under extreme peer pressure. She pushed me to join the basketball and volleyball teams. To my surprise, I found I loved to play.

College life made a new me. Sports taught me how to be a team player. We did not have NCAA-level games in China.

The official purpose of college sports was to make students active and healthy. Instead we played inter-department competitions, just for fun. The library science team was often the winner of women's competitions. Our homeroom wall was always fully decorated with sports or performance award certificates.

Working in America, once in a while I would throw something from a distance into a garbage can and often got "good throw" cheers from coworkers. I would say, "I played basketball in school." They immediately looked at me with disbelief. "You are so short!"

It was true that I was only 5' 5", but by Chinese standards that was not particularly short for a woman.

The academic workload was intense. The library science major was designed for a bachelor's degree completed in four years, but the education authority decided to speed up and condense it into two years. There were no library science graduates in Shanghai at the time and many research institutes were eager to get graduates to manage their book collections.

To me, math and science were more complex than the other subjects. The learning opportunities I had missed during the insane years of the Cultural Revolution were such a waste. Who should bear the responsibility? Only the citizen who was born in the wrong times. Fortunately, we had an excellent teacher from Fudan University's mathematics department.

Professor Hua was a young man in his late thirties, sharp and down to earth. He had an amazing ability to explain and prove complicated math problems in an easy way that everyone could understand, including me. Students liked him.

The title of Professor was not allowed in school during the Revolution. Instead, we called our math master "Teacher Hua." His job was to bring us all up to the level of college math required. To instruct such uneven-level classes in college mathematics was almost impossible, but he did! His blackboard writing style was clean and neat. It helped me to follow his notes easily. With him as the instructor, I loved math and loved his class, even though it was challenging.

One day, I was chatting with Teacher Hua after his class, he told me that he had worked at Tibet University for two years as a volunteer professor. To reach the capital city of Lhasa, he had first taken the train from Shanghai to a small town in Gansu Providence, a providence in Northwest of China next to Tibet. He rested for a day to adjust for the high altitude sickness, then took different buses to continue his journey. When he arrived at Lhasa, he was exhausted. The whole trip from his hometown Shanghai had taken him a week.

Mr. Hua was proud of what he had achieved in his teaching. For the very first time in history, he had brought young Tibetan men and women to the math level of trigonometry. It was the highest level they'd ever reached.

I did not understand. "Why didn't they study on a more advanced level? Aren't they smart enough to learn?"

"No, they are just as smart as you and me," Mr. Hua replied quickly. "But the people who live there were never taught anything like that."

He did not make big money by doing it. To help educate the Tibetans was a passion of his. He enjoyed teaching and being with young people much more than the money he made. I admired him.

No wonder he was so good at teaching us—the most uneven-level class ever at the university, I believed. Mr. Hua was one of the best math professors I have ever had. The students loved him with all their hearts. As it is said, "A teacher may not remember every student, but every student always has a teacher in mind whom they will always remember."

CHAPTER 17

THE LIBRARIAN

My college years flew by. Soon, no matter how much I did not want to leave, it was time to say goodbye to some of the happiest years in my life.

My mother passed away during my summer vacation. It happened so fast. Her cancer spread to her lungs and turned to the worse very quickly. As the first time, I realized that life was so fragile. She was only sixty-nine years old. It was the saddest time in my life.

As always, my school distributed jobs for graduates. Just like at high school, it was up to the university to announce where we were going. As I wrapped up my studies, I was informed that I would start working at an institution's library for engineering design.

My first day at my job was exciting but nerve-racking. It was a chilly and sunny winter day. As I rode my bike to the firm, a strong gust of wind tried to blow me all the way back home. Passing by familiar streets, I zigzagged through the cars and the people who were nimbly rushing to their various destinations—a typical life picture of Shanghainese in the morning. A mixed breakfast aroma with scallion pancakes and fried dumplings was dancing in the air.

I joined the bike flows in the narrow cobbled pathways and the wide boulevards. Squeezing between buses and cars sometimes gave me a cold sweat, but I was a veteran cyclist. Like a goat jumping on rugged mountains, I knew how to navigate the traffic with safety in mind.

Finally, half an hour later, I arrived in front of a high-rise Western office building on the Bund. Having parked my bike neatly in the employee bike parking alley, I stepped into a massive entry hall and looked around. With golden morning sunlight pouring through the huge front door and windows, there was a chandelier hanging from the high ceilings. The large entry room looked grand. The building was facing the Huangpu River, the largest river in central Shanghai.

I walked up to the second floor of the Information Department to meet my new boss. Mr. Hao was a tall man in his late fifties, burly with a full head of salt and pepper hair, wearing a pair of metallic silver-edged glasses. He looked like a refined gentleman as he stepped out of his office, welcoming me with both his large strong hands. The enthusiasm in the exchange was very kind and overwhelming to me.

Mr. Hao was the head of this Department, of which the library was a part. He took me on a tour of the whole floor. From one office to another, everybody was quiet and concentrated on their work. I was impressed and excited.

During my days in the factory workshop in the Revolution, with my hands covered in black oil every day, I had never imagined becoming a librarian in a research institute. Once again, I realized how important it is to regain an education, even if it had been lost long ago and was not perfect.

Since I was born, my life had always gone with the political swing of the country's Communist power struggles. I had been swept up and down in whatever direction the wind blew. Everyone had to learn to be nimble to survive.

I had never thought I would be able to overcome my status as a "bad-blood" kid and be able to work with books every day. Now, I felt it was a privilege and reward. I was busy at work every day but never bored. I was happy and satisfied with my new job.

The library was small compared to the rest of the research institution with its hundreds of employees. It had four small work sections, staffed by nine people. My position in the library was cataloger. Quickly, I made friends with everyone and felt I fitted in naturally.

My office window overlooked the bustling Huangpu River in the east, located in a busy district of Shanghai but was very quiet inside. When I moved to the U.S. years later and worked at the Port Authority of New York and New Jersey library on the 54th floor of the World Trade Center, it felt familiar.

Sometimes as I rode my bike to the office, passing by all the high buildings in the Bund, I thought of the colonial period of Shanghai before I was born. Being a colony of Western countries was like a double-edged sword. On the one hand, the Chinese culture and sovereignty were taken over by foreigners, but on the other hand, they pushed for cultural and economic exchange. Shanghai was like a living museum of all the key periods of Chinese history, from the emperor to the colony to the republic. The architecture of the Bund was a living record of this.

Winter in Shanghai was bone-chillingly cold. My office building had built-in heating systems. However, the government had a rule: any place south of the Yangtze River was not allowed to use heat in the winter. That included Shanghai. So, no matter the temperature, we had to suffer the cold environment indoors. Like many other people, I had frostbite on both hands and feet every winter.

Six months later, the old chief librarian retired and I was promoted to that position. Mr. Hao hoped I would lead and make positive changes for the library.

It was the winter of 1981. After eight years of dating, Yichin and I decided to get married. The wedding was the day after the Chinese New Year because people did not have vacation days. They used holidays for all kinds of celebrations. During that years, a religious service was not allowed for marriage ceremony. The wedding reception was held in a hotel with several ballrooms. The photographer asked us to take some pictures with both sides of the family. After my mother passed away from cancer, Dad never got remarried. When my dad came to be photographed, he was seated by himself as a single father. I saw tears in his eyes. He missed my mother.

Not long after being promoted to chief librarian, I found myself pregnant. It was a happy news to everyone around me but not to my department head. I saw the disappointment in Mr. Hao's eyes. Unavoidably, I had to take maternity leave soon. We still worked shoulder to shoulder together, but I felt a different attitude toward me. I got fewer requests to attend meetings at work.

I felt a familiar hurt from when I was a little girl during the Cultural Revolution. Back then, I had been dismissed from all leadership positions in my school because of my father's situation. The feeling of helplessness had pained me all over again.

To be a Chinese was not easy; to be a Chinese woman was extra difficult in such kind of situation. Now, as a girl of twenty-seven, what could I do? Bearing children was a woman's job from God, and I had to tolerate the situation. I could not ask my husband to get pregnant for me. Maybe Mr. Hao regretted that he had not hired a male librarian. With all the effort and energy I put into my job, I felt that life was unfair for women. That was a disturbing feeling it hurt.

At the end of the year, the library was named the "Best Working Group of the Year" in the company for the first time. I felt excited and proud of my job as the head librarian. However, I still realized the pressure as a soon-to-be mother. Even Shanghai, the most modern city in all of China, was still a man's world in 1982.

To be a first-time mother was not simple. It was a 24/7 job. Everyone tried to teach me how to be a mother. My aunt told me that before I touched the baby, I must wash my hands first. The visiting nurse told me to feed the baby every three hours and give her water between the feeds. My godmother saw how hard my daughter cried for food and told me that whenever the baby cried, I should let her eat. The housekeeper told me that if the baby cried nonstop at night, putting a broom behind the door of her room would bring peace. For all of that advice, my aunt's and my godmother's instructions worked the best.

After I had my baby, I, as first time, understood how much hard work both my mothers had put in for me. I could never thank them enough. One day when my daughter Crystal was about two months old, as I was breastfeeding her in my arms, I noticed she was staring at me with her deep, clear eyes as if trying hard to memorize my face. I will never forget the expression on her face, which touched my heart. I saw the eagerness to learn, the raw and pure love from a child to her mother. It washed out all the tiredness I had been storing up since the day I gave birth. It was my reward for being a mother.

After six months of maternity leave, I returned to work full-time. Like the motor company, the institute offered childcare service benefits to its employees. I was fighting with myself over whether I should bring my baby to the onsite daycare or not.

It would be challenging in the early morning. The bus was the only transportation available then. Public transport was so crowded on working days. The conductor often had to come down to push passengers to close the door. With a little baby, it would be impossible for me to commute by bus. Yichin was still in college as a final-year student, so he could not help. I did not see a way to bring my baby to childcare.

After a lot of debating, I decided to leave Crystal at home with our housekeeper. She was a woman with a big heart in her sixties, short but strongly built, with her gray hair neatly tucked behind her ears. Like many country peasant women, she came to Shanghai in her twenties and worked as a professional housekeeper. She soon became like another family member to me, just like my own nanny, Lin.

My life was hectic and stressful as a working mother with a six-month-old baby girl and a full-time job. Besides my day job in the library, every night I had to get up and take care of Crystal, feed her, and put her back to sleep. I am naturally a short sleeper. Six hours would be enough. However, all my friends were surprised to hear me keep complaining about sleep deprivation during my first year as a mother.

Our housekeeper had the same sweet Suzhou accent as my grandmother. She was from the same rural area where my grandmother grew up, but she did not make me think of Grandma because she was humble and never tried to give me orders. We called her Aryi, a nickname for a housekeeper in Shanghainese dialogue. Aryi was an excellent cook and could make any Chinese dish I named.

At her family home in the countryside, she had a husband and a married son. As she said, money was essential to her but not the only reason she wanted to be with us in Shanghai. Having worked in the city since she was a young girl, Aryi loved the colorful life and was used to the busy metropolitan world, even as a servant. She preferred to be away and send money back home as a breadwinner.

I never understood her relationship with the man she married. Her husband seemed a nice man on the few occasions he visited her. I did not know if Aryi loved him. As a traditional woman in that era, she just did what she had to: keep her marriage alive and support her family. Aryi did visit her family in the village a few times a year, but she always returned to our home quickly.

After my mother passed away when I was twenty-four years old, Aryi took the role of the leading woman in our family. I was happy to let her make decisions. Little by little, she became a part of our family.

Every evening when I got home from work, Aryi would have already prepared dinner. All my family enjoyed her cooking very much. Sometimes, my dad had visitors from Hong Kong. They would remember she was an excellent cook and inquire about her preparing their feast.

Dinner time was the family's happy time. While eating, Aryi would tirelessly tell me what adorable things Crystal had said and done when I was at work. My daughter was the princess and the center of the family's attention every day. Dinner was like family entertainment, the most enjoyable time of the day.

After I moved to the U.S., people often asked me if the Chinese discriminated against my baby girl. I would look at them as if they had six heads. "No. I have never seen it."

However, on second thoughts, I told myself that China was so big. The cultural development and progress of civilization can be very different from region to region. Shanghai was the most modernized city on the great map of China—it was closer to the outside world and more Westernized than any other part of the country. The news media was only allowed to report censored news. The average citizen had no choice but to believe the voice of the government-controlled news outlets. The TV and newspapers were very strictly monitored. Listening to any American radio, such as the Voice of America, could be a crime. The newspaper might never report abuses against little girls. How could I know the truth?

I can only say that *I* never saw baby girls mistreated. To my knowledge, none of my friends or my friends' friends ever had such an experience. In my family, my daughter was spoiled rotten.

Life was smiling at me again; everyone envied my job and life. But to people's surprise, I was thinking of changing again.

I wanted to see the outside world and go on the road my uncle and auntie had traveled before they returned to China. I wanted to give it a try. Like them, I wanted to go to the United States.

When Crystal was four years old, Yichin was admitted to a US college for a master's program. I encouraged him to go, but we had no money. Even though it was a US state university, in 1985, $2,000 a semester for tuition was considerable for us, the survivors of the Cultural Revolution. My father contributed $150, all the U.S. dollars he had saved after the 1966 raid. The government only allowed each person to exchange $30 for going to the U.S. The tuition had to be prepaid in order to get a student visa. What could we do?

My father wrote to relatives in the U.S. for help. All my cousins had their families to support and could not help us financially. At this important time, my cousin Irene, Uncle Wei Zuo's oldest daughter, agreed to loan the first-semester tuition to Yichin. She was an English teacher, not rich, but she took the risk to help me, a relative whom she had never met. What made her make this sacrifice? I always wanted to know but never received a straightforward answer from anybody.

In a traditional Chinese family, when an uncle seriously asks for help with money, he should get consideration and support. This is a special kind of cultural spirit that exists between Chinese families and relatives' networks. It was the same as when my grandmother helped Lin—Grandmother expanded our family network and included Lin, whom she loved and sympathized with. It was the trust and the willingness to help each other that made us a family.

My father and I pledged to return the money, but I did not even know where we would get the funds for the second-semester tuition. There was no way I could raise the two years of college expenses altogether then. Yichin decided to borrow the first-semester tuition from Irene to pay for the school so that he could get his visa, then go to the U.S. during the summer vacation to work and try to earn enough to cover his living expenses before the class started in September. When there was an opportunity, one had to take the risk. I cannot thank Irene enough—every time I look back on the obstacles we faced, I know that her important contribution made our dream possible.

At the time Yichin left for America, Crystal had reached kindergarten age. As an only child myself, I knew she needed to socialize with other kids. I was very pleased to see in the first week of kindergarten that she made friends like a small fish swimming in a large pond. But her exciting new life also brought problems. She got sick from other kids in school easily. I was constantly in the children's hospital emergency room.

This was a difficult time for me as a young working mother. I felt overwhelming pressure. At work, I often worried about whether my baby was OK; at home, I often worried about work. My unbalanced life sent me into a guilty circle that never went away from my mind. I learned that to be a good mother, I had to pay the price. Sometimes, it could be an expensive price.

At night, no matter how tired, I had to get up at midnight to feed my daughter; in the morning, I was always the first to jump out of bed. Sometimes, Crystal would wake up and stare at me when I tried to sneak out to work. She thought that I must have abandoned her and would cry as hard as she could. It was always challenging for me to deal with the morning scene. The sadness of her screaming broke my heart, but I had no choice but to go, though I felt sad and guilty the rest of the day at work.

No young mother was staying home watching the baby then; looking after kids was the grandparents' job, according to Chinese culture. Even today in China, most grandparents are the free babysitters for the next generation if one is lucky enough. If not, many families hire nannies or pay for daycare. Life for a young mother is just like that.

As a book lover, I bought a pile of how-to books for my new role. One of the books instructed that in such a morning situation, the mother should leave her baby without looking back, even just slamming the door and going. Then the child would learn this was non-negotiable and accept it as a daily routine.

I closed my eyes and ears, held my breath, and just did as the book said: leave. It needed a strong mind. Believe it or not, it worked well. Soon my daughter was fine in the morning.

China was pushing the One Child policy in the '80s. A second child was not allowed. The government gave families a lot of small rewards to encourage them to give birth only once, and there were government networks to watch the families in every neighborhood.

The family planning ladies would come to my house without warning on weekdays. These ladies lived in the neighborhood and knew every possible mother-to-be very well. One day when I was at work, they came to my house and asked Aryi what kind of birth control method I was using. How could she know?

Aryi was smart and handled it well. She promised them that I would not want to have a second child because I was already struggling between work and home life. It was true. The planning women had to report the answers to the higher authority. They seemed satisfied with the response and left. When Yichin left for the U.S. for grad school in 1986 and I took the job of taking care of my daughter solo, the event I was afraid of the most was Crystal getting seriously ill.

My second-floor neighbors were a lovely couple with two young kids. We shared a kitchen with them, always chatting together while cooking. They both had jobs at a power company and worked alternate shifts. My mother used to watch their kids for free when they were too busy. Neighbors helping each other were always accessible.

One day in the kitchen as we were cooking, the man approached me and said, "I know Yichin is leaving for the U.S. soon. Don't worry. If Crystal gets sick at night, please feel free to knock on our door, even if it is midnight. I will go with you to the hospital. Please don't feel hesitant."

In those days, the taxi was not popular. To get to the hospital, I would have had to hold a sick kid in my arms and walk two blocks to the bus stop then walk more blocks to the hospital when I got off the bus. It was a tough job for a woman. A man's arms were necessary. To a single mother like me, this offer of help was priceless.

Our neighbor was sincere and repeatedly reminded me of that offer afterwards. Fortunately, I never needed to ask for his help. Thank God, Crystal was four years old by that time and getting stronger.

Chinese people did not have much money in the '80s, but they were closer and helped each other more frequently and selflessly. Nowadays, I see families living in private dwellings, hardly knowing what their next-door neighbor looks like. This makes me sad. Human beings are social animals. Care and love for each other were more easily found in the Shanghai of my youth than in modern life today. Actions of love and kindness brought the community together and made life a joy, even during difficult times.

China continued its reopening to the world in the 1980s. As time went on, I heard more and more stories about the U.S. from people around me, as well as from my uncle and auntie. People were feeling freer to express their thoughts.

Uncle visited the U.S. in the 1940s as a visiting scholar, and Auntie told me about her Columbia student life in New York. The ironic thing was that they always were careful with their word choice, as if they were talking about a lousy enemy when they mentioned the U.S., but their stories were not as vicious as expected. People were still afraid that the government would punish them for what they said. The memory of the Cultural Revolution remained as vivid as if it had happened yesterday.

However, our conversations about the outside world always gave me the opposite impression of what the government intended. They still called the U.S. imperialists, even though the Vietnam War had ended many years ago. However, it always sounded interesting when real people told me their real U.S. stories.

I often talked with some foreign exchange students in the libraries. Their experiences drew me more and more to this far and mysterious country. The image the government had put into my head and the image from other people's experiences were somehow different. I did not know whom to believe. Maybe I should trust my cousin who lived in the States or the college student who was doing research in the library. I had many questions about America in my mind but could not get many answers.

China was still isolated from the rest of the world. There were no real news resources. Listening to American radio stations was prohibited. I told myself: I must see the U.S. by myself and give it a try.

After a one-year separation, I decided to join Yichin in New Jersey. He was taking classes during the day and working at a restaurant at night to support himself. Without a doubt, I thought that we should be together as a family regardless of whether we were rich or poor. But Yichin insisted on not bringing our daughter with me.

The reason was that his college was not located in a good area. The kindergarten was not sound. We did not have money to send Crystal to a private school. Yichin thought she would be better looked after by any of her grandparents.

It was a tough decision. I went back and forth with him on the long-distance phone line with a big phone bill and little progress.

No older generation could help me to take care of Crystal. My father had never cared for any child and had no experience. He was a social butterfly and liked to hang out with his friends during the day. He also volunteered for some activities related to his job. My mother-in-law promised to help me but found that she did not have the energy to watch Crystal full-time. They were widows and widowers living alone. I understood and respected their decisions.

At this difficult point in my life, Auntie and Uncle, who never had a child, stepped forward.

One Sunday, they came to our house for a routine visit. Uncle sat on a bench next to the piano while Auntie stood behind him. They talked about the decision they had just made. Crystal would be under their care when I was in the U.S. They were excited but nervous about the new duty they were about to have. I had never dreamed they would do this for me, but with the influences they had given me as a child, I was convinced that it was the best plan for my daughter.

The traditional Chinese culture does not have hugs and kisses or anything to express love in day-to-day life. Holding feelings within oneself was the norm and considered polite. I did not know how to react on that day and was too excited to say anything. I am sure they understood my appreciation well because they knew the culture better than I did. If I could redo it today, I would give them the biggest kiss and hug, which would melt their hearts away. They were like angels sent from the heavens to me. I could not ask for anyone more perfect to take care of my child than them.

No matter how fortunate and blessed I felt, packing and leaving my family, and the city I grew up in was not easy. My father was in his early eighties. He loved to have me around but supported my decision to go. My dad was the most prominent supporter.

Crystal always loved to stay in my auntie's apartment overnight. To move in was not a difficult task for her. She could not wait for the long-term sleepover, even though I wouldn't be there. She helped me pack her favorite toys and was ready to be a first grader at six years old.

Looking back, whether I was a librarian, a college student, or an assembly worker in a motor company, I always sought change. I dreamed of going to America one day but never thought it could be true.

Life is filled with challenges and opportunities. Grab them when they pass by. If you set your goal in your heart profoundly, the seeds will grow. If you stick to your dream firmly and never give up, you will reach your goals. The persistence may pay off, believe me.

When I left Shanghai, I had no idea what my life would be. The new world could be good or bad, but I wanted to take the risk and see it through my own eyes and judge it by myself, not by what the government told me.

Moving to the U.S. was never all about money to me. My family was OK economically. It was more about seeking a life with freedom and ideologies that were very different from old-fashioned Chinese culture. The dream opened my eyes as a little girl, and now I was a grown woman, looking forward to taking my own journey to the U.S.

PART II

CHAPTER 18

GOING TO AMERICA

The Boeing 707 finally landed on the runway of JFK Airport. People were exhausted after the eighteen-hour flight and could not wait to rush out. The voice of the airport's speaker was announcing something, but the American English accent was quite different from the British one I was accustomed to hearing in China. All by myself in a foreign airport, I felt nervous.

My trip halfway across the earth from Shanghai to New York was my first flight ever. I looked at the vast hall, and it was overwhelming.

The customs officer at the inspection point looked suspiciously at my super-size luggage. Frowning, he asked, "Miss, what is inside?"

I replied, "Oh, just a lot of clothes." Yichin's school welcome book to international students said that clothes were costly in the U.S. and to bring plenty.

He did not say anything but signaled for me to pass.

As I exited with my two large suitcases, the first thing I saw was my husband waving to me from the waiting area. He was thrilled to see me and took my luggage immediately. We hadn't seen each other for over a year. It was a happy, exciting, and bittersweet moment. I missed my daughter and wished she was with me.

Quickly, Yichin introduced me to his friend, who had driven him there to pick me up, as Yichin did not have a car. The guy was a graduate student in his class, tall and thin with an easy smile. I was delighted to see another person from my country in this unfamiliar city.

The car brought us to an old apartment building in Newark, the largest city in northern New Jersey. The apartment was in a three-story red-brick building in need of updating. Our unit was small but big enough for the two of us. It was located next to Yichin's college. It was also next to a hospital, so ambulance sirens rang in my ears day and night.

I told myself to be flexible and patient. We were new here. Things would get better.

Soon after I arrived, I started working as a waitress at a Chinese restaurant. Yichin needed money for his next semester's tuition. He went to classes during the day and worked weekend shifts to give me a break.

I met many Chinese college students, as I lived near the school. Most of them came from Taiwan and China. Like me, they had been as spoiled as princes or princesses by their parents back home, but they were learning hard work and self-reliance in this new country. Life was not easy; they struggled to balance academia with supporting themselves, but all were happy to be here.

After settling down, I started to explore the city I now lived in. The local population was mainly minorities, black and Hispanic specifically. It was the first time in my life living closely with races other than Chinese. It felt like I had suddenly moved to another planet and was weird at first, but soon I got used to it. Everyone seemed to mind their own business and mostly got along.

The block I lived on was lined with student fraternity houses. Every Friday, when I finished restaurant work and returned home at midnight, the parties were just getting started. Seeing people happily having fun I could not help recalling my student life in China. We only studied and studied. I was jealous—life would be very different if you could choose where to be born.

One day after shopping, I was downtown waiting for a bus. As the bus approached, people moved forward to get on. I felt someone push me from behind. I immediately looked for my wallet, which was suddenly gone. In Shanghai, there were always security guards at storefronts warning people to carry purses in front of them. I was trained to be alert from a very young age.

Immediately, I looked around. A young woman was hiding her hand behind her body. I knew without seeing it that my red wallet was in her hand!

Within a heartbeat, I yelled, "That is my wallet! Give it to me!"

As fast as I used to react on the basketball court, I grabbed my wallet back. The woman was so shameless—she smiled without embarrassment while everyone watched us as if watching a show. We continued riding on the same bus as if nothing had happened.

This incident occurred so fast. It told me that the U.S. was not very safe and to be alert to crime even during the daytime.

If this episode had happened in Shanghai, the pickpocket would have gotten beaten to the ground by passersby. In the 1980s, there were no credit cards in China. If a thief got someone's wallet, there might be a whole month's salary inside, needed to support a family. Strangers on a bus would have come to help even before a police officer could get there. People hated stealing so much.

In the streets of Newark, there was no cop around. As a new arrival, I did not know the correct way to react. I did it without much thought.

The fact that no one acted in response was a new cultural shock to me. I told myself this was another country. People cared about themselves more. I started using credit cards and not carrying large sums of cash.

While I was getting familiar with my new life in the U.S., Yichin graduated and started working as a software engineer in downtown New York. Having a professional job meant that he could choose to stay in America if he wanted to. But he was not sure then. While he was a student, we had only lived in Newark and hadn't seen any other part of the country. The crime rate was high and it felt unsafe to raise a family there.

We used to have a stable life in China: we were not rich, but we never worried about safety or job security and we had free access to healthcare etc. The violence in Newark made him hesitate. He wanted to see more of the new country before making a decision.

I will never forget the clear, sunny morning of June 4, 1989. I was driving to go grocery shopping, and on the radio I kept hearing *peng-peng-peng*, the sounds of gunshots. The

Tiananmen Square incident had begun. It was a live report from Beijing. The killing had only just started.

What should I do with my daughter back in Shanghai? I watched the news very closely and had sleepless nights. My uncle and auntie took the best care of her. Crystal continued her piano lessons after I'd left. She started when she was four years old and now had begun playing recitals on stage in public performances. Every time I called home, she was always happy. It seemed to me that my daughter adopted her new life well and did not need me anymore. I was a little jealous, but more, I was happy for my daughter. Uncle and Auntie filled my role perfectly and loved her with all their hearts, sometimes even doing a better job than I could. Crystal became part of their life, and in so doing, added extreme happiness to their life without her quite knowing it.

The Tiananmen Square massacre put a dark, heavy cloud over me. I was very worried. What would happen if the relationship between China and the U.S. soured again, as it had over the past thirty years since 1949, or even got worse?

I remembered the sad story of Uncle Wei Zuo and my grandmother. After 1949, when the Communists took over China, they never again saw each other. I felt a chill go down my spine at the thought of never seeing my family in China again.

The belief that parents and children belong together whether they're rich or poor was a value held deep in my soul. I could be happy with less money, but love had to be shared. No matter how hard life was, a family must be together.

I persuaded my husband to bring Crystal to live with us. When the news traveled to Shanghai, it broke my father's heart.

He loved Crystal dearly and did not want her to go. She was his only grandchild, the princess of his world, and the center of every family member's life. Now I was far away in the U.S. The situation was taking the source of their fun and happiness away.

However, I still insisted on Crystal going to the U.S. Dad, my uncle, and my aunt did not say anything to prevent it but started preparing for Crystal's journey. They were selfless and understanding, always considering others' interests first. It was one of my family's traits. It was and still is priceless to me.

CHAPTER 19

CRYSTAL'S NEW WORLD

My uncle decided that only Aunt could have the job of accompanying Crystal to the U.S. Auntie was an amazing woman who would give her life to protect Crystal and I was sure of this.

My aunt and Crystal's first stop in the U.S. was San Francisco to see Uncle Wei Zuo and his family. Auntie had not seen them since 1948. Uncle W. Zuo had been the general manager of the Grand Hotel Taipei for thirty years before he retired and moved to a suburban area near San Jose with his three daughters.

It was overwhelming when I was introduced by my cousin Irene to dozens of family members. The Christmas dinner was held in my cousin Ivy's house, which had a large dining room overlooking a kidney-shaped swimming pool in a beautiful garden. When my dad visited them years ago, he performed tai chi by the water every morning and loved it.

It was my first formal Christmas dinner in the U.S. Ivy prepared two styles of food to satisfy all family members' appetites. There was spaghetti with meatballs for those who loved Italian food, and cold noodles with sesame soy sauce for those who preferred Chinese. The latter option was primarily for the older generation of Chinese relatives. It was a reminder that eating habits were hard to change and we'd better respect them.

Of course, there was also smoked ham for everyone. I had never met any of these people before. After Mao took over China in 1949, there was no mail service between the island and mainland China. Now we were in the same room enjoying the reunion, which was actually the very first meeting. I felt incredible. The big family of Uncle Wei Zuo, his children, and grandchildren had all moved to the U.S. Everyone was so excited about the party and the Christmas holiday.

Seeing that happiness on everyone's face, I wished my grandmother was there. She had loved and missed her dear son Wei Zuo so much.

As soon as the holiday was over, Auntie, Crystal, and I continued to our final destination: New Jersey. We lived in a small town called Kearny between Newark and Jersey City, not far from Manhattan.

The City of New York was breathtakingly gorgeous with holiday decorations and exuded happiness. The Big Apple was the best welcome gift for a seven-year-old girl in her new world. For the very first time, Crystal got a lot of Christmas gifts from an old man she'd never met, Santa Claus, who placed her presents under a tree. That was a character unknown in Chinese culture then. Christmas was not a holiday on the Chinese calendar. We never celebrated it in Shanghai.

Crystal didn't know what Christmas was, and staring at a pile of her gifts, she asked me, "Mom, why does Santa love me so much?"

"Because you were a good girl in the past year," I said with a mysterious smile.

With confusion on her face, she did not say a word. Everything was new and exciting for her. As a child at the winter wonderland, she loved it.

School started right after New Year's Day. On Crystal's first day, I was nervous, because she did not speak English. The few words she understood were learned from my aunt and uncle when they used the language at home.

The school was a short walk from our apartment. At 3 pm, Auntie left to pick her up. I could not wait and ran out to meet them in the stairway.

"How was your school today?" I was anxious to know.

"I don't know what they were talking about in English. But the math was like in kindergarten," Crystal answered without looking at me.

In Shanghai, kids her age, seven years old, had already learned the multiplication tables in school. Addition and subtraction were taught in kindergarten. Here in the U.S., she was repeating it and felt bored.

Knowing she was newly arrived from another country, the school principal assigned a Chinese girl to help Crystal get familiar with her surroundings. She spoke Mandarin, the same as Crystal, and had moved from Taiwan years ago. They soon became best friends.

One day I received a notice from Crystal's school about a parent–teacher meeting. Growing up in a teacher's family, my mom and auntie always took the parents' meetings seriously. I always tried to learn to be a parent from my parents. Like them, I prepared dinner early that day.

The State of New Jersey required children not from English-speaking families to take an ESL (English as Second Language) class for at least one year. When I arrived at the meeting that evening, I met Crystal's ESL teacher, a young blond lady with green eyes who projected warmth. She introduced herself to the parents and gave us an overview of the class. When the meeting was finished, she pulled me aside for a private chat.

"Hello, are you Mrs. Jiang, Crystal's mother?" the teacher asked with a sweet smile. "Crystal told me that you helped her to learn English. Can you tell me how you helped her?"

I looked at her with surprise written on my face. "I did not help her. I don't know why the kid said that…"

Crystal picked up English quickly, even though we only spoke Chinese at home. Less than two months after her arrival in the U.S., I overheard her reciting the Pledge of Allegiance to my aunt one day. I could not distinguish any difference between her pronunciation and that of an American-born kid. Children were supposed to pick up languages faster than adults, so I thought her progress must be typical.

The teacher did not give up. "Oh, come on, you are the mother. You must know how."

I tried to think harder for a while and said, "The only thing I can think of is that I always borrowed children's books from the public library every week. She enjoyed reading and loved them all. I returned them by the next week and got another book pile for her." I hardly ever read them with her because I was busy taking some English and computer classes at the local university and working part-time.

The teacher was satisfied and nodded: "Yes, you are right. And also because she wants to learn. Some children will not listen to me if they don't understand what I am saying, but Crystal always tries to listen. She raises her hand sometimes. That is what matters. If every kid were like Crystal, my job would be much easier."

We both laughed. I will never forget her as a good teacher, loving her job and the kids both with all her heart. When Crystal was in high school, she got many national awards. Some committees asked me to nominate a favorite teacher who influenced the child. I thought of the ESL teacher. It was not fair that the elementary school teachers never got this kind of opportunity. I drove back to her school to look for the ESL teacher. Unfortunately, I was told she had got married and left the school. I never found her. She had probably changed her name after marriage.

The place we lived then was a blue-collar town. Crystal met a lot of working-class children and made good friends. Many parents did not speak English, but they were good and hard-working people. I invited their kids to birthday parties, and Crystal joined them at home or church celebrations. I was very pleased to be able to experience diverse cultures.

My next-door neighbor Mary was a super-friendly and devoted Christian in her fifties who had grown up in the Midwest. Mary had seven kids from two marriages. Her youngest daughter, Anna, was one year older than Crystal. They played together after school. Mary did not like the local public school. Every morning, she drove all her kids to a private Christian school ten miles away from home, then picked them up in the evening. Her husband worked on Wall Street and had no problem supporting a big family. She loved to help and always showed me how to handle problems. As a new immigrant, there were too many things I did not know. To me, Mary was an encyclopedia.

If my car could not start, I would call Mary. If my apartment was too hot or too cold, I would call Mary. If I could not find the vegetable I wanted in the grocery store, I would call Mary. Sometimes, she would send her husband to my home to help me. Mary taught me everything about living in the U.S. and even in the world. I felt so lucky to have her next door. We were good friends.

In the summer, Mary took her seven kids to their summer vacation house on Long Island. She often asked if I would let Crystal go with them. Crystal loved to go there. She enjoyed playing at the beach on Long Island with Anna and the other kids, who were like her siblings. In the meantime, Anna learned to speak some Chinese words from Crystal. Mary used to call Crystal her #8 child and joked, "Make sure when Anna comes home, she must speak English, please."

Crystal's English was getting much better with every passing day, but it still needed improvement. I had one simple requirement for her overnight trips to Long Island: She had to write me an essay about her trip every time. Writing was an essential skill in life. It helped one not only in grammar, structure, and organization of sentences but also in logical thinking. Crystal was always happy to promise me that. When I read her descriptions, I enjoyed her experience as well. She called Mary and her husband Mom and Dad in the articles. I thought they were too. All the kids had fun and enjoyed each other as good companies.

When Crystal reached nine years old, Mary showed me a brochure of a Christian summer camp in upstate New York and asked if I would like to send Crystal there. She had volunteered to cook for the camp. Her seven children would be there with her during the two weeks.

The summer camp was located at a beautiful Native American reservation near Buffalo, New York. It had a pond in the front and a substantial green mountain in the back. Showers were outdoors. Everyone lived in a row of rustic wooden cabins with no air conditioning, very close to nature.

For the first time, I was not sure if Crystal would be homesick. Mary suggested I register her for one week in case she wanted to go home, so I did.

When I picked her up at the camp after seven days, I could not recognize that this happy dark-skinned girl was my little princess. The first words she said to me were: "Mom, you should have booked me for two weeks."

"Why? You missed me, didn't you?" I asked with my eyes wide open.

"We had competitions every day. If I stay through the next week, I will win awards, like swimming. I am very good at it now." She pointed out the muddy pond and showed her tanned little arms with pride.

However, Crystal did get one award for other activities than swimming. They were rewarded with sleeping on the mountaintop under the stars and cooking breakfast by using flint to make a fire. She was thrilled and did not miss home at all!

I looked at my little girl, her skin was healthy red-brown from playing under the sun every day. It shone more under the bright daylight. What a difference between her summer life here and the one she used to have in China.

If we had stayed in Shanghai, Crystal would probably play the piano every day, do her summer homework, and take a daily nap: the mandatory summer routine for kids. My daughter was not the same girl today she had been when she arrived at JFK Airport last Christmas. She was like a little bird who had left her mom to explore the woods for the first time and was excited to fly a longer distance. A tiny Chinese bird migrated to a new continent. She did not know what fear was. I released the door and ensured that a cage did not numb my baby's wings. I felt proud as a mother bird.

Our small town was about twenty minutes' drive from New York City. Living near so many world-class learning resources was a blessing. As a librarian and book lover, I took Crystal to many museums and parks on weekends. She enjoyed the Bronx Zoo most and loved it at first sight.

As an immigrant, everything was new to me. I sometimes looked at the animal over the fence in the zoo while reading the description. In my head, I was quickly searching for the Chinese name of the animal I might have seen in school. Unfortunately, most of the time, I couldn't recognize it. I would ask Yichin, "Do you know this animal's name in Chinese?"

He was silent, which meant he did not know it either.

Crystal couldn't understand why I bothered to ask such silly questions. She pointed to the furry little cutie and said, "This is better than a dictionary. Why do you still ask, 'What is it?'"

All of a sudden, I lost the ability to explain the reason to my seven-year-old. As an adult from another side of the earth, I preferred to have it translated into my language. I could not learn a new concept in the same way as a child did.

While everyone got used to our new life, I realized the school was a bit too boring for Crystal and she hardly had anything to do after class. Watching TV and playing computer games were the main activities for passing the time. Her math was always at the top of the class, but she did not learn anything new.

One night, I attended another parent–teacher meeting. There was a father who was complaining that math was too difficult for his boy. While the math teacher tried defending the class, the father said it might not be difficult for the teacher but could be too difficult for the kids.

I learned for the first time that American schools were very different from their counterparts in China. In Shanghai, the education department set the academic standards for every grade and gave them to the teachers to work from. If that class did not reach those standards, it would be the teacher's responsibility. In addition, teachers were greatly respected by the culture. No parent should ever question a teacher's criticisms of their kids. This education structure pushed all students to perform at close to the same level.

I decided to change Crystal's school. There were only a few options in the area, and they were all Catholic schools. Changing the school district meant moving. I had just settled down and got familiar with the area. Plus, it could give immense stress to little kids to move too often.

And if we did move, where should we go? I did my school research at my library using reference books, paper, and a pen. After reading the school reports and looking at census data, I realized that the towns that had great public schools were all too expensive for us.

Yichin just started to work in New York after graduation. We did not have much money saved. What should I do? I could either put Crystal in a small private Catholic school or wait a few years, then move to a good school district.

I consulted Mary and her husband. They were our best American culture advisors and were very understanding and loving. I was convinced that high school was more important than elementary for children. If we moved out before Crystal hit high school, she would be fine to catch up. We did not have much money to buy a house or pay for a private school. I decided to wait and save.

CHAPTER 20

THE LEAFY TOWN

Spring came and went. Two years had passed since we had settled in the U.S. I'd got used to living in this town, which was convenient to commute to my job in downtown New York. Every morning I walked to the train station in twenty minutes, whether rain or snow, jumping on the train to my library in the World Trade Center.

However, the school system was weighing on my mind. I started searching for a house in our price range. Every weekend, the three of us jumped into the car, touring different areas. Behind me, Crystal carried her Cabbage Patch doll along with us. She was busily examining her room too. With a good school system as an essential in my mind, the research led us to some expensive neighborhoods.

At lunch break in my library on weekdays, I reviewed the research I had done at the weekend again. I could not give up my priority: the school system. Many friends advised me not to be too picky; average schools were OK for a kid.

Facing mountains of information, I felt as if I had gotten lost in a big woods and did not know how to find the path leading to my destination. I told myself that I could stay in a smaller house, but my child must have the best education. When my baby grew up, I never wanted her to feel that because of her mother's decision, she had not had the same advantages her friends had. I tried to make up for my lost opportunity. She deserved to have the best opportunity, as every American child did.

At that time, Yichin's company asked if he would like them to sponsor him to apply for a Green Card, giving him the right to permanent U.S. residence. Without hesitation, I voted yes. Why not? We all liked our life in this country.

After months of house hunting, I found a home close to schools and downtown in a leafy suburban town about ten miles from Kearny. The house was simple, but the school system was one of the best in the State of New Jersey and topped the national shortlist as well. The asking price was a little over our budget. Regardless of the price tag, I wanted to give it a try.

Mortgage processing was confusing and complicated. In the '80s, there were hardly any people buying homes in China with mortgages. Most people were renters, like my family. Those who did buy houses mostly paid cash from their bank accounts.

Acquiring a house was a brand new experience for me, and I was learning. I worked hard every weekend to collect the paperwork the bank required, and then I waited. When the approval date came, we received a surprising letter: "Denied."

Why? The mortgage advisor never gave me any warning about possible rejection. I was shocked. I would have used another bank to speed up the processing time if we knew it was possible to be denied. The bank told us later that the reason for denial was that I'd worked in the U.S. for only two years. My working history was not long enough to be counted as credible.

We were devastated. This was in the '90s, before the subprime mortgage financial crisis.

So, we started again from square one. Yichin walked into a small community bank downtown and filled out a new application, and then we waited. I warned the new bank that I only had two years of working history in the U.S., but they seemed not to care.

A few weeks later, after dinner, I was washing the dishes when a man came with a thick folder and rang the doorbell. He was a middle-aged gentleman with thin, dark brown hair, friendly and sharp. He was the loan officer from the new bank and had come to meet us for our new mortgage application.

I seated him at our kitchen table and served tea. After ten minutes of chatting, I found out that he lived in the town next to where our new house was located. Also, he was an economics professor at Yichin's school in New Jersey and was moonlighting for the bank. Soon we became old friends as if we had known each other for a long time.

Quickly reviewing our file, he looked at both of us and asked, "Why do you want to purchase a house in that town?"

I stared at him, not understanding what he meant.

He saw the expression on my face and explained. "I meant there are so many other places in New Jersey: Why did you guys choose that town which it's further away from New York, where you both work?" He did not point out that this was a more expensive community.

I replied at once, "It is the school system. I did a lot of research and found it is one of the best in New Jersey." He looked at me for a second, then nodded and kept making notes. As a professor, he knew more about the importance of education than anyone.

"You will get your mortgage." He closed his folder. The meeting was over.

I looked at him with disbelief. "How do you know we can get it? I did not work long enough in the U.S. to meet the three years mortgage requirement."

"But you did work at restaurants on and off. I will add the days together. It is enough." He did the math in his head and said it with confidence.

As he promised, we got the mortgage commitment the following week. It was a life-changing move.

I said goodbye to Mary and my other neighbors. Mary asked me if the house was worth the money we would pay. She did not have her usual smile on her face.

I answered without hesitation: "Yes, absolutely."

She did not say anything, a little sad in her eyes to see me leave. I was too. She wished me good luck. We hugged. It was a sad moment for me to let a dear friend go.

We moved into our house in mid-October. Millburn was a lovely suburban town with a train line linked to New York City. Many people worked in the city, where the money was.

Life here was very different from the urban town we used to live in. Houses were much larger; the yards were cut much neater and were greater in size, with well-planted flower beds. I hardly ever met people walking on the streets but only saw them drive past, usually in a Mercedes-Benz.

It was a different world. Would I fit in here?

As a city girl from Shanghai, I had never seen a red October, and I found this leafy town breathtakingly beautiful. Crystal's elementary school was not too far away from our house. It was in a magnificent English mansion with red bricks and white wood trim, well maintained.

The leaves were in their peak season. When I walked my daughter to school in the mornings, the whole scene was just like an elegant oil painting of autumn under the golden early sunshine. Looking around the campus, kids were happily walking to their classrooms. Most of them were around the age when my elementary education was stopped.

Looking at the leaves closely, I remembered a children's book I used to love when I was a kid. The little painters with wings flew around to paint the leaves in the striking colors in the fall. Some of the painters overturned their palettes or buckets by accident, messing up the color! That was why some leaves were part red and part green or yellow…

Watching the rich-colored street scenes day in and day out was a pleasure. There were very few red trees in Shanghai. The popular French planes covered most of the streets of Shanghai with their yellow leaves and arches in autumn. The trees were a symbol of the French culture imported into China. They were eyewitnesses to the establishment of the Shanghai French Quarter in the '40s. The planes were indeed stylish and full of personality, but they were very different from the stunning red in northern New Jersey.

Crystal was not happy for the first few weeks in her new home. She missed her friends from her school in Kearny.

During the first month, she kept asking me to move back to our old apartment. I pretended not to hear her.

As time went on, we explored more of this leafy community. Downtown was ten minutes away. We could walk to stores. Every day in our backyard, we saw squirrels, rabbits, and sometimes even deer. That made Crystal yell loudly with joy periodically. She enjoyed having the animals for company while home alone after school. This was a new experience for her as an urban girl. After a while, I stopped hearing about the moving back request.

We had left our first hometown, Shanghai; we had left our second hometown, Kearny; now, we were trying to adopt our third hometown here in northern New Jersey.

My next-door neighbor was a retired man who came to see me one day. "Welcome to the neighborhood." That added great warmth to my new life in the unfamiliar block. I was the only Asian around.

The man was excited to tell me about his impressions of the Chinese. He used to live in New York City, where he'd had a Chinese neighbor who owned a laundromat and was a hardworking guy. His children had been well-behaved. *He must think that we are all the same.* I smiled and expressed my appreciation, telling him I was terrible at ironing and just learning laundry as I moved to America. He was surprised at first, but then we both laughed. I did not tell him my housekeeper spoiled me.

I might have disappointed his view of a stereotypical Chinese woman, but the truth was that every human being was uniquely distinct. The U.S. immigrant's life had taught me to be self-reliant and know who I was.

Even in a town so close to New York City, it needed a lot of cultural bridges to navigate the differences between East and West. Many people saw me as the first Asian woman in their life, and I felt I had to ensure my behavior gave a good impression to my American neighbors.

Crystal's new class was all Caucasian, with one Chinese boy. In Shanghai, there was only one race in schools. I tried not to let her feel that she was different from her friends. To have her blend in with her peers and become a member of the community was a priority.

When the summer came, I found life in Millburn was very different from our previous blue-collar style of living. Most of the kids here left home for their summer camps; others traveled out of the country with their parents on family vacations. Some went to their summer home in New England or a beach house on the Jersey shore. Crystal was one of the lonely few left in town while I was working.

Without hesitation, I planned a road trip to Canada. To see Niagara Falls in person had been one of my long-time wishes since I was a kid. Uncle had told me a story about when he came to the U.S. as a visiting scholar in the 1940s. He met a lot of top research scientists, many of whom were Christians. One of these close friends told Uncle that he became a believer in God when he visited Niagara Falls. Only God could create this kind of magnificent scenery. Really? I wanted to see the Falls with my own eyes and to feel the shock that man experienced.

The following summer, we drove to Ottawa, Montreal, and Quebec City. Yichin was a homebody, never enthusiastic about travel. He preferred to stay home alone and play handyman, but I put him in the driver's seat anyway.

To everyone's surprise, after the first trip, he suddenly became an enthusiast of travel and couldn't wait to go the next trip. I could not believe it.

A lot of Canadians spoke French as their official language. I picked up a little French vocabulary before the trip, but reading the highway signs while driving was really challenging. Remember that was an era before GPS was invented. I was the navigator for Yichin, sitting in the passenger seat, trying to translate the signs into English as fast as possible.

One day, we were looking for a bridge to the other side of the river. We headed back and forth several times, frustrated.

I was saying to myself, "Can't find the bridge, only see *Pont*."

Crystal was sitting in the backseat quietly. Suddenly, she yelled out, "*Pont* is bridge in French!"

Good girl! My baby was growing to be my teacher. We laughed together. If English was my second language, French would eventually get to be my third.

Since we could not afford to go to Europe on vacation, the Canadian cities pulled us closer to European culture without the price of a long-distance flight.

The lengthy hours of road trips also brought us closer as a family. In the car, it allowed me to discuss some topics that Crystal might not like to listen to. On an average day at home, she could walk out of some of my "lectures" to another room. But in the car, she had to tolerant me.

I found that was the best time to discuss unwelcome sub-jects with Crystal, like quitting a sports team or boyfriend. More important, travel opens a kid's eyes and teaches adults to be flexible and accept different cultures while understanding the world better.

Together we learned a lot on the road trips.

CHAPTER 21

THE BALANCE OF LIFE

Another year passed by. We were getting used to our life in the suburban. Crystal became a middle school student. Millburn had one middle school and six elementary schools. The sixth graders from the different elementary schools were suddenly entering a much larger school all together. The middle school campus was more extensive than a small community college. There was an overpass thoughtfully designed for students to safely cross to the fields on the other side of main Street.

Crystal just got used to her small element school, now she was trying to survive with the new middle school environment. In the early days she often got lost in the huge school building while looking for the next period classroom. There was no time to go to the locker, so she had to carry all her textbooks, running from one class to another. Quickly, she became familiar with her new school life, made many new friends, joined the field hockey team.

This was a traditional wealthy town. Most mothers did not work. I was one of the very few who worked full-time, but Crystal could always manage to have someone drive her home on a bad weather day. She knew how to survive.

One snowy morning, the school called every family to let them know they would be opening late. I left for work at my usual time, and so did Yichin.

At dinner time, Crystal was sad: "Today, every one of my friends had parents drop them off. I was the only one who walked to school." She looked unhappy.

I felt awful but tried not to show it. "No, it is impossible. Someone must have walked to school too. You didn't know."

"No one! I asked everybody in school. They said they were sorry for me," she said with stubbornness in her eyes.

I felt my stomach turning. I wished I was a stay-at-home mom like the women in my neighborhood. As a parent, I always wanted my daughter to feel no different from her peers. What could I do?

Every morning I had to take the 7:30 train to work. The school changed its opening time to 10 am due to snow on short notice. Yichin stayed home later the next day to drive Crystal to school.

As soon as Yichin walked in at 7:30 pm, he smile, "You don't need to worry about it. The kids weren't cold. They were fighting to each other with snowballs all over the streets this morning. They were having fun."

I realized that I might be overreacting as the only working mother on the block.

A few weeks after her middle school began, I started getting calls from Crystal's teachers during working hours. Each of them asked me if I would allow my daughter to step up into an honor class. Of course Crystal should if she qualified. I believe that the higher standard you set for a child, the harder they will try to meet it. It is always better in the learning process. I asked myself, was it supposed to be a question for me?

If this kind of thing happened in China, parents could not say "Yes" quickly enough. When I was a young girl, there was no such category as an honor group in school. We all studied at one level. Sometimes, I got bored listening to the teacher and began talking softly to the kid sitting next to me. At the end of each semester, the school sent report cards to every family. Opening my school report, my mother would read similar comments every time: "Had too many unnecessary talks with other student…in classes." I was only discussing the problems that my teacher raised in the lecture, nothing else!

After moving to Millburn, I soon started feeling the pressure of commuting. It took me more than an hour and a half from home to my library on the 54th floor of the World Trade Center in New York. Sometimes the train had signal problems and would stop in the middle of the route for a long time.

What could I do? This was the new life I had to face. I wanted to be a good mother, a good worker, and good at everything simultaneously. I believed I could do it.

Every night after supper, I prepared the next day's dinner and put the half-readied food neatly back in the fridge. The next evening, when I hit home, I immediately started cooking. As if I inherited the gift of being a fast cook from my godmother, within half an hour, I would have a hot, delicious, home-made meal for the three of us on the table ready for Yichin coming home.

For all the years, I never had a meal late at dinner time. Life was hectic, but I was happy to make my family happy, as my mother said that shared happiness was twice as good as happiness alone.

A neighbor who lived on my block saw me leaving home early every morning and said with a smile, "Nowadays, young mothers have to work because they carry big mortgages." He was in his late sixties and probably remembered that when his kids were small, his wife did not need to work. I waved back with a smile, then continued hurrying to catch my train. He was right. I did feel the mortgage was heavy on my shoulders.

Crystal was an easy kid to raise, just like my grandmother used to say about me. She loved all kinds of foods, but I tried to change the dinner menu every day so that she would not get tired of the same thing. Eating a nutritious and varied diet was very important for me as a cook, mother and the manager of this small family.

The United States was also a good school for teaching me what life is. I never cooked in China, because we always had a housekeeper. Coming to the U.S., I bought a lot of cookbooks and started learning. Soon I could easily cook for a dinner party. Books were my silent teacher. Self-learning was amazingly useful, as my uncle had taught me. Life as an immigrant taught me much more than I could ever imagine.

Comparing with the Chinese middle school, the life here was colorful and fun. The students held a dance party every Friday evening in the school cafeteria. They loved it.

One day I saw Crystal was holding hands with a boy while walking on the street. John was a tall twelve-year-old, the same age as Crystal. He was one of her classmates and dancing partner at the Friday dance. He was polite and sweet, a good student of English literature, from a family with four siblings.

I was surprised but happy for them as well. The early puppy love was cute, though I was a little bit worried about their young age. It would have been prohibited in China. When I was seventeen years old, in high school, dating was a "crime"; when I was eighteen years old, as an apprentice in the motor factory, dating was prohibited as well. The reason was always: it will take too much time and energy away from learning. It was considered a waste of time.

However, the authorities could not lock love out of young people's hearts. We learned to go underground, never admitting dating but always referring to it as friendship. There were always excuses that could be found to justify a friendship. The young people knew how to get away with it. They were far smarter than the authorities at handling things like this. Many of us only met on our dates during weekend breaks.

If twelve-year-olds were found to be dating in China, it would be a big crime. The school would interfere and punish the student. I called my aunt in Shanghai and told her Crystal had a boyfriend. She was an educator and must know how to handle it, I thought.

"Really? Oh my God!" Aunt yelled at the other end of the telephone line from Shanghai with big surprise in her voice.

"Yeah, Auntie, it is OK. Many kids here do have dates. I just want to share it with you, you know." Compared to her voice, I was calmer.

Aunt did not say anything more. She loved Crystal. However, the Chinese culture was deeply entrenched in her mind, having moved back to China in 1949. I had to choose what to do myself.

I wanted my child to appreciate the rich culture, the quality of the education, and the freedom she had here. She must utilize it completely. I also thought that, as a young girl, she should enjoy her teenage life completely. The puppy love should be part of her experience as a teen. Why not let her be? With clear memories of my own, now it was my daughter's turn. I wanted her to be happy, happier than I was, the happiest girl in the world if possible. She got much more freedom than I did in high school. My right to have dating experience as a teen was taken away. Why should I take that right away from her? I wanted my child to grow freely, like a young tree developing to its full shape of its own with the benefits of the sun and rain.

I told my aunt not to worry about it, I would handle it.

When I mentioned to Auntie that she used to follow my boyfriend and me to check we weren't doing anything too intimate, my memory made Auntie irritated. She looked at me from the side of her eyes and said, "OK, Crystal is your daughter. I will not say anything."

Aunt was an American/Chinese, half and half lady. She was deeply influenced by the classic Chinese tradition, learned in childhood and at her undergraduate medical school. At the same time, her powerful affection for America, which grew out of her time at Yenching University, Peking Union Medical College and Columbia University in the '40s, was like a powerful tornado that blew another half of her Chinese philosophy out of her mind without her control. When she returned to Shanghai from New York, she brought Western democracy to our traditional family. Unlike my grandmother, Aunt did not want to be a queen. She was an angel with invisible wings, always putting Uncle's and others' interests in front of her own. She gave me the total freedom to raise my child. Auntie passed away in Shanghai in her mid-nineties, and we all love and miss her dearly.

Long before I came to America, I heard lot of fascinating stories about this faraway country, especially at home from my uncle and aunt. They told me the good and the bad, the happiness and the sadness.

It was like putting yeast into a dough: when time passed and the temperature was right, the dough would ferment and grow bigger. The idea of freedom grew in my mind without being noticed. Saying things good about the United States in public was forbidden, but the positive impression was implanted inside of me. It was growing little by little every day.

I wanted to go to America to see this country by myself.

Once in a while, I got caught up in thoughts of "American cultural invasion," which was a theory rooted from the Chinese Communists. In the 19th and 20th centuries, some Christian missionaries and their schools, under the protection of the Western powers, went on to play a major role in the Westernization of China. Yenching University (now Peking University) and the Peking Union Medical College with its Hospital were a few major ones. Yenching was sponsored by the Christian churches back in the U.S. and the Boxer Indemnity. The Union Medical College was founded by Rockefeller Foundation. Most of the professors were from America. They brought modern education to a large population in a poor developing country, importing Western culture, science and freedom along with it.

The Peking Union Medical College trained a lot of world top medical professionals in China. Even some Communist Party leaders after the 1949 "liberation" had them as their personal physicians.

If this is "cultural imperialism," it must be a good thing. The U.S. influence was very positive and powerful because it was brought by education and medicine. It greatly helped heal the Chinese people when they needed it most in the 1940s.

It was way more powerful than a military invasion. The schools and the hospital America invested in produced love, not hatred.

I am sure, just like me, the younger generation of the doctors, patients and staff will always look at America and Christianity with special personal views, no matter what they were told to think. The lives the hospital saved and the good education the schools brought to this country will live in Chinese people's hearts forever.

Today, the medical school and the hospital still bear one of the best names in China. It will never fade because Mr. John Leighton Stuart brought excellent education with love for young intelligence. People will always appreciate the ideologies of equality, love, and humanity that he passed around through the generation.

The political and cultural influence of the schools was irresistible. *Time* magazine once called Mr. Stuart "perhaps the most respected American in China." I am not sure if it was from God's help, but a part of the funding to support the Yenching University came from donations from the Christian community in the U.S. and U.K. If this is a so-called cultural invasion, then it changes the world in a more peaceful way than a wartime invasion.

War not only kills lives but also plants the seeds of hatred generation after generation. Cultural invasion, on the other hand, spreads sweet seeds of education and help, then harvests love.

Maybe we should think twice before we decide to bomb another country next time.

CHAPTER 22

AN IMMIGRANT MOTHER

One day, Crystal came home from middle school and said, "Mom, the teacher tried to scare us again. They said high school is going to be really hard." With a sly, disbelieving smile, she added, "They said the same thing to us when we were going to middle school three years ago. It wasn't bad at all."

"Oh, really?" I said while folding my laundry. "But I think you'd better prepare for it well, hon."

Crystal's school life had been filled with changes. Moving from Shanghai to a blue-collar urban town in America was a big step for her, then to the suburbs. Making friends and adapting to the new cultural environment was not easy. However, middle school was a tipping point. She quickly adjusted and stayed in a positive mood.

After we first moved to Millburn in October, I had attended the first one-to-one parent–teacher meeting at Crystal's new elementary school. Her teacher was a petite Jewish lady in her late sixties with thin red hair and large eyes. She was competent and a straightforward speaker.

Offering me a seat in her classroom chair, she looked at me though the top of her reading glasses. "How many times have you moved since Crystal arrived in the U.S.?"

"Once. This was the first time." *Does it matter?* I asked myself. Knowing that moving was stressful for a child, I always tried to avoid it at any cost. That was why I had not moved her to the Catholic school in Kearny.

"I know Crystal was an honor student in her old school, but she may not be on the honor roll here. Are you OK with that?" She was fast to her point.

"No problem. I understand. If she could make at the top of her class next year, I would be pleased," I replied from the bottom of my heart. Any school change was not easy for kids, but as a mom, I hoped she would catch up quickly.

"Crystal sometimes makes mistakes in grammar tense. Have you noticed?"

"Yes. She did. Because the Chinese language doesn't have grammar tense," I said, "We speak Chinese at home. Yes, I made the same mistake once in a while too." It was true.

I was confident that Crystal would be perfect in her new language soon. No matter how difficult it was, being bilingual was what I wanted for my daughter. Children should be able to jog between a few languages easily. It would benefit her over the course of her life. I insisted on speaking Chinese at home with Mandarin occasionally, Shanghainese, and English.

"Oh, I see." The teacher nodded. "Every week, I give my students a vocabulary list to memorize. It will help them with SATs in high school. I think you can utilize it with Crystal."

I felt a little bit uncomfortable. Did she think I was only at fifth-grade level? Immediately, my second thought came up: maybe it was true—I might be only at elementary level in

English. Sometimes I would spell words wrong, especially if the term had a foreign root from another language, like zucchini.

"Sure, I will. Thanks for the suggestion," I said with a smile. Why not?

Later on, I learned this teacher was well known for her students being good at wide ranges of vocabulary when they were in higher grades.

The academic difference between our old town and this new school system was a warm-up exercise for Crystal. It made her feel that the challenges from graduating from elementary to middle school were not a big deal. She got accustomed to adjusting quickly from school to school.

The year Crystal entered high school, my uncle passed away. It was a desperately sad time for our entire family. I wanted to help my auntie to cope with it. Knowing she missed Crystal very much, I invited her to stay with us for a change and tried to distract her from the sadness. She agreed.

Looking at Crystal's curriculum, Auntie, a retired high school teacher of thirty years, was shocked to see this public high school was so outstanding and similar to a key high school in Shanghai, which meant it had a high standard with a very competitive curriculum.

The Shanghai public school system was similar to the New York City public school system. The Stuyvesant high school in New York City would be an example of a key high school in Shanghai. They were basically the feeders for top universities in the nation, but it was hard to get in, requiring students to pass an entry exam.

As soon as the fall semester began, high school sports teams started recruiting freshman athletes. Crystal was busy making her choices. I suggested volleyball because I had played it in college. It was fun. Despite the fact that she had no sports training, many coaches welcomed her in. One day, after school, she came home and said, "Mom, some girls were crying because they could not get on the volleyball team. I even don't care to be on it."

"Oh, you are in the team?" I hadn't expected that, because she had never played it before.

"Yes, I am in JV now," she replied. JV meant junior varsity, a feeder for the varsity team in the future years.

"Great. Listen to me. I think that you should join three sports this year, one each for the fall, winter and spring seasons. You will be able to see what you are good at later on. Then drop one sport every year until the junior year. You will have a spot on your best team. When you apply to college, you can show your best sports marks on your application. Does that make sense, hon?"

"Yeah, maybe," Crystal answered with reluctance. College seemed a long way away for her still.

Growing up in Shanghai, sports were never an essential item on a student's report card; neither did parents encourage kids to play. In Chinese society, there was nothing more important than academics. I saw the significant cultural differences between the two countries. I told myself to try being an excellent bilateral cultural mother accordingly. Being an immigrant, *adjusting yourself is an essential job.*

The high school fencing team was among the best in New Jersey. Crystal was interested in joining. Again, the coach accepted her on the spot. She started her training with the school team equipment as a trial.

One afternoon, Crystal came home after practice with worry in her eyes. "Mom, the coach is sending me to the match tomorrow. I do not know much about fencing yet; I don't even know how to hold my weapon right."

I did not know either. We had no fencer in our family. However, I could not show my lack of knowledge. Mom was supposed to be omnipotent. I had to encourage her however I could.

"Don't worry about it, dear. Fencing is all about strategy. You can pretend to hit her right side while quickly attacking her left." I made all this up on the spot.

Crystal listened and did not say anything. The next day their team won the match. She lost her bout but was excited to be able to get her feet wet on the strip. She loved the experience of being a swordswoman.

Shortly after this, her coach called and suggested I send her to private lessons. He gave me information about personal coaches and clubs. I ordered her a complete set of weapons and uniforms. She was thrilled to be a varsity fencer.

Soon, I found myself as busy as a taxi driver, on the road either to the New York fencing clubs in the evening or to matches on weekends. This was in the days before GPS, internet, or cellphones. If there was a fencing match at the weekend, I had to call the hosting school for directions the night before. I never knew why, but the girl's games were always held at 8 am on Sunday mornings. Crystal's weapon, the foil, was always the first on the schedule.

We would get up at 6 am, have a small breakfast, and be on our way to the hosting school. Fencing was a winter sport. Half of the time, when I left my warm home, the roads were covered with snow. No one was on the streets.

I had to drive carefully. If I made a wrong turn and got lost, there was nobody I could ask for directions. People were sleeping on early Sunday mornings in winter. Somehow, we always got there. Thank God.

Yichin was a conventional Chinese dad who did not think kids' school sports were important and loved to sleep. I was the driver and left him alone to enjoy his Sunday. He would clean the house and cook dinner before we came home at 5 pm. That was a typical Sunday in the winter fencing season.

Crystal's coach had suggested she go to a New York fencing club to practice because they had better fencers than our New Jersey ones. Every Wednesday was our scheduled day in New York City.

On a typical day, I would arrive home from work at 5:05 pm. Crystal would be waiting for me in front of our house. As soon as I pulled into the driveway, she would jump in with her fencing gear and backpack. When I started driving, she started doing her homework in the car. By the time we arrived at the Holland Tunnel, the crossing to Manhattan, it was totally dark. She would put her work away. When I approached the fencing club at 23rd Street, she would go upstairs to the practice room herself. Sometimes, we had pizza nearby. Then I would park my car and go to the Barnes & Noble bookstore across the street to read. The book parlor had a lot of interesting author lectures.

I enjoyed the precious time to relax. When she finished at 9:15 pm, we would drive home for more dinner.

Raising a kid also enriched my learning experience in this new country. Being a working mother was not easy, but it also contained sweet and precious moments. I miss that evening time in Manhattan as a fencing mother.

Every so often, I had to travel with Crystal to national competitions when her high school was in session. She missed classes, but it didn't seem to be a problem. Crystal's name was in local newspapers from time to time. I did not read the sports sections, but our neighbors cut the articles out of the paper and collected them for her.

The ladies in my office were very supportive. Some of them even suggested raising funds for Crystal to go national. This was something I did not see in China often. It touched me deep down in my heart. The love and care were overwhelming.

In contrast, nobody paid any attention Crystal's academic achievements, although she was a top student. Neighbors were excited for her and recognized her only as a sports star. For all the years we lived here, only one man congratulated me on her school performance. He lived next door to a family Crystal babysat for. Besides him, it seemed to me that no one ever cared.

This was a surprising cultural difference between China and the U.S. If we had lived in Shanghai, people would congratulate me on my child's school performance only. No one would care about sports awards. Only the national college exam scores would send a young person to the best college. Nothing else mattered.

It was another big culture shock I had to absorb after moving to the U.S. People in different parts of the world could value their life in different ways. I don't know which is better than another.

I found myself standing at the crossing of the intersection of cultural conflicts. I was confused and surprised by the arrows pointing in opposite directions. I was willing to change myself for good, and wanted to be both a politically and a culturally correct mom, if that were possible.

Also, I was moved by the love and admiration of Crystal's buddies. They were her loyal fans. She first learned fencing as a freshman in high school and soon got seeded at the top in the State of New Jersey. Her story sent a powerful message to all the kids: If a school transfer, an immigrant, could do it, they could do it too.

Most of the kids in the neighborhood were just like their parents. They ignored their friend's academic performance but treated Crystal like a sports hero. Being an athlete was cooler than being a nerd. At least in my town it was.

In winter, when fencing was in full swing, the varsity fencers were very busy. There were matches and practice every day. If it was an away match, the school bus would be back in town at 9 pm. Then she came home to shower, eat dinner and do homework. When Crystal went to bed, I was already asleep.

At Millburn High School, classes were dismissed at 2:30, but in the massive gym, the excitement was just beginning. The smell of sweat was floating in the air. It was a sign of hard work. I cherished the teenage lifestyle here. It was amazingly different from that of Chinese teens.

However, the academics were still very demanding in all four years of this top-rated public high school. The full sports schedules plus all AP classes taught Crystal time management well. Often, I saw her sitting on the strip floor between the bouts doing homework. The noise in the gym was so loud, you had to yell to be heard, but it did not bother her, nor did it bother other athletes. They would take out a pen, a book and concentrate on their homework. I think sports were excellent training for kids. It was not only building character but also teaching them to be mentally strong and manage their time. It would benefit their whole life. Chinese educators should look into it.

No one was more excited about Crystal's performance than my aunt. She had been a softball star in her university time in the 1940s. Not many women participated in sports then, but Auntie was a pioneer.

According to Uncle, she was the only woman in the school's history to receive the Sports Spirit Award. He joked about it and said she was too short to get the ball but very busy running around. Auntie did not like his joke and hit back. The Yenching school newspaper called her pitching a "magical serve." No one could catch it. I believe the training made Auntie an extraordinary woman: a hard worker, a team player, desperately wanting to win, and always ready for challenges. Of course, Auntie was Crystal's biggest fan. When she was staying with us, she watched every one of her field hockey matches and tried to be her coach sometimes.

Crystal was a member of the school varsity volleyball team. At the high school matches, I often saw the kids cheer for

Crystal on the court. I tried to imagine how good Auntie had been when she was young. I remember that once in college, I threw the ball into the basket in a competition, and the whole court was calling my name. It was an exciting moment, but I only remember that one time for the honor. Now, my daughter had her friends cheer her name in the games all the time. She was my hero.

An old Chinese proverb says that indigo comes from the color blue but is more beautiful than the original blue. My child is a better me, thanks to the diversified education environment.

At the weekends, I tried to be the "Mom's Taxi" driver for the kids as much as I could. The other mothers took the duty for me on weekdays.

When I grew up in China, volunteering was an unknown concept. Everyone tried only to mention their own business, nothing else. The Cultural Revolution made people focus on trying to survive and protect themselves.

In New Jersey, our local hospital had a department to manage the young volunteers from nearby schools. Most of them were from the high school in our town. Crystal passed her first interview in life with the hospital volunteer department, happily getting her pink and white candy striper outfit. For many of the kids, this was an honorable tradition handed down from their grandmother or great-grandmother. The hospital offered the kids bagels after school to work there. At the end of the year, they had fun parties to celebrate the good work that had been done. I looked at my daughter and envied that she had this meaningful experience.

On my journey from Shanghai to New Jersey, I learned that it was alright to look at the world with different eyes and always be ready to learn and accept new ideologies.

The high school junior and senior proms encouraged the kids to have dates and socialize together. Crystal still hung out with her boyfriend, John, from middle school. As long as she had a good standing with her academics, I was mostly OK with her dating, though sometimes it still got on my nerves, regardless of how open-minded I tried to be.

John was a well-mannered boy. I liked him when they came to our house occasionally. In fact, I liked all her friends. She picked her friends well.

Like most families in town, John's had a summer house down the Jersey shore, about an hour away. On summer days, they often went to the beach house for fun. They were swimming, kayaking, and playing on the beach. Crystal loved to go, just like she used to go with Mary's family to their Long Island home. Everyone loves the ocean and the sun in summer.

One day after dinner, I was watching the news on TV when Crystal came to me. "Mom, can I go with John to their beach house this Saturday to stay overnight?"

I looked at her and asked, "Why must you stay overnight? I prefer you sleep at home, sweetie."

She immediately understood my worries. "Because no one can drive me back home that night. Nothing will happen, Mom. I promise you. Can I go, please?"

It was a clear sky summer night. The moon was like a shining plate hanging outside the kitchen window in the dark background. I sat at the table with a blue and white tablecloth in a checker pattern.

I thought for a while and knew it would be a difficult talk, but I had to do it.

Pointing to a line on the tablecloth with my left hand, I said, "Look, this is the line you should never cross." Then, I used my right hand to draw a line to create an area: "This is the dangerous zone. I know, maybe nothing is going to happen, but I don't want to take chances."

Crystal got irritated; she still wanted to go. The next day, she did not talk to me, nor the day after.

I stuck with my decision stubbornly. To be a responsible mother, unfortunately, one had to make unpopular decisions on many occasions.

The weekend approached, but she did not ask me again. Later, I learned that the boy's mother had canceled the trip. Thank God. I got off the hook.

CHAPTER 23

AMERICAN STYLE

Learning to be an American mother was the main ingredient of my colorful immigrant life in this leafy town. Different from most Chinese parents around here, I did not send my child to the piano lessons, or the Chinese school on weekends. No body cared about the way I taught my kid. This is America. I loved the freedom to be a mother of my own choice.

Unlike in China, kids do not have summer vacation homework in the U.S. Crystal enjoyed her free summertime, despite a list of summer reading. Just like the poem, she wrote, "Summer is cool, absolutely no school…" She loved her American life and could not be happier.

Reading books was her favorite thing to do. It did not count as "work." Within a month, she had finished the original list and started reading more books from our local library.

In this town, a family vacation was a regular household activity, a culture. However, I never had the opportunity to have a vacation in China. When I worked at the factory, I often dreamed of going traveling, but nobody I knew had such time away from work. When people around you do not have it, you can tolerate and accept it. *Vacation* must be a foreign word in a Chinese dictionary.

While I was working at the factory, one of my relatives invited me to go to Beijing on October 1, China's National Day. Because people did not have vacation days, we used the national holidays to travel or celebrate weddings.

A few weeks before that, I handed my request to my boss. He had to grant his permission before I could take days off and leave Shanghai. Unluckily, my boss called his boss to check. His boss said no because Beijing would be too crowded on holiday, because of me! They turned me down. I was so sad, as well as furious. The capital city would always be crowded during holidays. Living in a country that did not allow for vacation was a pain.

I had been all packed and ready to go. That was my first opportunity to travel in life, and I was so looking forward to going. The reason for my rejection was so ridiculous! And there was no place I could appeal. To be Chinese, you had to obey. I never requested any travel permission after that. I just gave up.

But going to see the world was still firmly planted in my heart. Vacation should be a fundamental human right. I do not know why *travel for leisure* was not written in the culture book of Communist China. Maybe they were afraid it would inspire thoughts of individual freedom or encourage open minds.

The philosophy applied to Chinese citizens was always "Put the nation's benefits first." Then who would care for the interest of an individual?

My uncle used to quote a famous Chinese author, Lao She: "I love my country, but who loves me?"

Now that I lived in the U.S., I could choose my lifestyle. The summer after Crystal's first year of high school, Auntie was visiting us. I rented a cottage on Lake Champlain in Vermont. As a new experiment for the whole family, the four of us stuck together day and night without TV, although we had a boat on the lake. It was a cozy two-bedroomed house with everything we needed. The New England summer was low humidity and very pleasant. Compared with the hot summer in Shanghai, it was heaven.

I witnessed the sunrise over the beautiful, mighty Lake Champlain from our living room every morning. With soft breezes, the sunlight nudged the mirror-like water into a wrinkled silky sheet. It was extra smooth and peaceful. So close to nature, I felt like I was a country girl again, but this time I was not working in the rice fields and had no pig dung in my hands.

With no stress from work and life, the four of us became even closer to each other. It made up for the family time I

Summer vacation in Vermont. Crystal and I playing water in a stream.

missed when I was busy at work, with no time to even chat. Precious days!

During the week, we visited the family home of the von Trapps from *The Sound of Music.* Now it was a hotel. Crystal loved to see the Vermont Teddy Bear Factory and the bear hospital, but Ben & Jerry's ice cream factory was the most beloved place of all. We relaxed while eating our ice cream under the stars.

Auntie enjoyed the slow pace of country living. She cooked dinner for us every day, letting me take a break. I brought a large box of seasoning from home and we had a delicious homemade meal every night. Without a computer, TV, phone, or GPS, I tasted how amazingly happy a simple life could be.

After dinner, Aunt cleaned up while I read a book, and Crystal and Yichin played cards or chess. Life was so sweet when it was pure and raw. Even Yichin, who did not like my plan initially, wanted to come back the following year. That trip made the vacation a family tradition forever. Everyone loved our week away from home and told me family time was priceless. Cherish it when we can.

When I was a teenager, I always felt like I was a second-class kid due to my father's status in the Cultural Revolution. I never recovered totally. The hurt would come back to me from time to time.

Luckily, I could choose what I wanted to do now. I want my daughter to be happier than me and enjoy the best the world could offer.

While I was busy learning to be an American mom, Crystal's college application process began.

I started my college visiting program during her freshman year in high school. I always tried to visit on a day when the high school was on holiday but the college was not, so we could not miss a class but see the university in session.

Meeting the students was just as important to me as seeing the buildings and talking to the faculty. The characteristics of student bodies told me a lot about the quality of the education the college could provide.

Before leaving for the first college visit, I called the high school guidance counselor for advice on which colleges would be suitable for my daughter to visit when we went on our summer vacation in New England.

The counselor picked up my call immediately and said, "Oh, Crystal is a top student in our school. She can apply for any college in the nation."

Really? I was truly surprised by her answer. When did my little duckling turn into a swan? I was always ready to help her at any point, but she had not needed it so far.

The first college I visited with Crystal was Princeton. I picked Martin Luther King, Jr. Day to go to, when the classes would be in session, and booked the group tour.

We drove down the highway and arrived at a beautiful, gothic-style campus one hour later. It was a chilly winter morning. As soon as I parked my car in the guest parking lot, passing along the tree-lined street, we got lost in the huge campus. Some students were walking by; I stopped one young lady and asked, "Excuse me. Where is the admissions office?"

She looked at me with an easy-going smile, then pointed to a faraway stone building and said: "There are three ways to get there. The first one, you go this way…"

I was stunned. What a complete answer to my simple question! She could have just told me one way to go. But instead, she let me be the boss with a map for my plan. I took a deep breath and thanked her. It is worth choosing a day to see students. I said to myself, "This school is too overwhelming for Crystal." I wished my daughter would be able to get in.

During this visit, I also stopped to see the school fencing coach. The gym was located on the outskirts of the campus. Many athletes were riding bikes there, but the main gym was empty because of the midterm exams. It was vast and modern. However, without the athletes, it looked lonely and cold to me. The head coach was a well-built man with a French accent, kind and polite.

He showed us around the facility and shared some statistics about the school varsity team members. It showed me that the athletes might not perform as well as the non-athlete students in terms of academic achievements when they were in school. The coach was warning me.

However, four years later, during the school graduation week, at the Varsity Club celebration dinner, a student athlete's research thesis showed all the guests that although an athlete may not have the best results during their school years, mostly they would achieve more in a lifetime than the students who had better scores in school.

All sports training at the university was voluntary. Coaches would not call students to be trained. They would have to come to the gym themselves. Academic work was the first priority. I was impressed.

I came to visit with great curiosity and returned home with much knowledge about the school in one day. It was worth the trip.

I never got a chance to visit any universities in China. There was no such culture. No college was open to prospective students. That probably made me more eager to see each school in the U.S.

I appreciated the opportunity to examine Ivy Leagues with my own eyes, especially with my student daughter. As a mother, it was essential to me to let her see and feel what the next four years of her life could look like and to help her prepare well. That responsibility drove me onward. With Crystal as my navigator, we saw more than a dozen colleges together.

During the visit, I learned what a world-class university should be. More importantly, I learned not to be afraid of challenges when the opportunity was there; I learned that anything was possible in the land of opportunity. If one worked hard, the gate would be open. The admissions people did not need to know whether a new student's father was capitalist or not, nor did the parents have to find a "back-door" connection to get in. Just try.

School visiting was a true learning process for me. It opened my eyes to a new world of education. If I had been born here, would I be a different person today?

Looking at Crystal, I wished I had had the same opportunity when I was eighteen. Looking at the people around me, especially the men and women near my age, I often wondered, what would they accomplish today if they grew up during the Cultural Revolution in China? Would they be a doctor or a professor? Or would they be factory workers or peasants like most of my high school classmates?

It breaks my heart to search for the answers sometimes. Why could life be so different from person to person? Bad things do happen suddenly in life, and often it is not that person's fault. People sometimes do not appreciate what they have until it is gone. My generation of Chinese youth did not get equal rights for primary education. I hope that will never happen again to any generation, regardless of race, age, or background.

After Crystal's high school guidance counselor's comment, we visited many best colleges in the nation. When Crystal went to national fencing tournaments on the west coast, we visited Stanford and UC Berkeley. Yichin joined us occasionally, though he was often busy at work and with house maintenance tasks.

Raising children is a challenging and complicated job, but it also rewarded me with opportunities to learn about other parts of life.

As a novice American mother, I managed, and we enjoyed vacations at Yellowstone, Grand Teton, Seattle, Alaska, Chattanooga, the Florida Keys, Miami, Palm Beach, California, Vancouver, Banff, Calgary, Ottawa, and Quebec City, etc. during Crystal's high school years. Without summer vacation homework, kids could learn more about life wholly and colorfully than I did with a summer homework assignment in China when I was a student.

CHAPTER 24

EDUCATED

The college applications were due in two weeks. One Saturday morning, I was in the kitchen doing something when Crystal called me with trouble written on her face. "Mom, so many questions to be answered on the forms. I don't know how to do it." She showed me a pile of application forms and paperwork.

"What's your problem, dear?" I asked.

"Look at this one. The question is: 'If you are given a position in the government, what kind of position would you like to have?' I don't know."

I didn't know either, but I had to pretend to know something, because mothers were supposed to know everything. "I think that is asking you what kind of changes you'd like to bring to the country. If I were you, I might want to be the Education Commissioner so that I could look into the inner-city school problems... and there is a lot that could be discussed. Isn't that good?"

She did not say anything, just walked back to the paperwork on her desk. I continued preparing my food for dinner.

Ten days passed. Crystal came to me again. "Mom, do you want to hear my answers to this school application?"

"Yeah, of course." I was anxious to hear.

She started reading her short essays for the application forms to me. I was surprised to learn that my baby girl wanted to be the President of the United States!

"Oh, it is great. But why didn't you like my suggestion?"

She looked at me with a puzzle, "Oh, what did you suggest?"

"I said Education Commissioner…"

"Sorry, I don't remember you saying…"

Why should I bother to be serious? She did not take her mom's words seriously. Is this anything new?

The other questions on the application forms interested me. "What is your favorite time of the day?"

She answered it easily: "3 am. Curled up in the corner of my room, reading a book." That was exactly her. Enjoy the quietness of the night and read.

Other questions were: "What kind of music do you like most?" and so on.

What intelligent questions the college admissions officers created! They were trying to figure out if the prospective students' personalities were the right fit. If they were not what they were looking for, an offer could be closed off. Personality matters a great deal. It helps a person to succeed.

As April 1 approached, every high school senior who had applied to college held their breath. Crystal was nervous too.

It was a Saturday morning. I stepped out to check the mailbox as usual. The mailman had left a pile of letters. Some were from colleges; some were junk mail.

When I walked with the mail stack to Crystal's bedroom at 11 am, she was still in bed. She looked at the letters, then gave them back to me and refused to open them herself.

"Mom, please open them for me."

The first was from Princeton. I read the acceptance letters and handed them to her to re-examine them. She jumped out of bed and gave me the biggest hug ever! Then she was on the phone with her friends all the time and did not need me anymore.

People often asked me how I helped my daughter get into an Ivy League school. The answer is that I didn't. I did not know why she got accepted by the school. Her SAT scores were not the highest in the applicant pool. I guessed her vibrant extra-curriculum activities helped. She might have answered some of her essay questions right, or she came across as one of the sleepless, overachieving kids the college was looking for.

As an immigrant lacking Western cultural background knowledge, and with English being my second language, I learned about the acceptance process via school visiting trips and reading college guidebooks. With great curiosity, I observed the process with common sense. I did everything an average mother could do.

During Crystal's high school years, I often heard people complain about racial discrimination in college admissions, especially toward Asians. I have asked myself numerous times: did I experience it? The suburb I lived in had very few Asian residents, basically all Caucasian at the time, though some were Jewish.

My honest answer is: No, I didn't. Maybe I was not sensitive enough to discrimination. I used to be significantly discriminated against by my own people in my teenage years just because my father was an entrepreneur. I was told I was born with bad blood in me. Since then, I have never tried to be a top student again. I obeyed my fate as a second-class child for the rest of my life.

Growing up, the dark shadow was always following me. How often had I told myself not to speak my mind? The impact of discrimination never left my heart, and it still hurts. I learned not to be the leading goose among the other geese because the hunters on the ground would shoot the leader first. Being an average follower will be much safer and easier.

Without noticing it, I lost the sharpness of competitive impulse little by little after that hot summer night in June 1966. It had a more significant impact on my life than I realized.

Every immigrant's child might have different experiences growing up in the U.S. It could be harder for some kids to adapt to a racially diverse environment than others. However, cultural diversification would not only teach children to be flexible and tolerant of others, but also open their minds to additional ideas. I hope all the children from different races and family backgrounds could feel as equal and happy as Crystal did in this country.

Princeton classes started in mid-September. It had a unique beginning for freshmen, which opened my eyes again.

At the end of August, Crystal chose to participate in a program for freshmen called Outdoor Action. The students could choose whether or not to join. They were assigned to different teams according to the hiking skills they stated on their application form.

For one week, the kids hiked in the mountains and valleys during the day and slept under the sky in a professional hiker's sleeping bag on the ground. They had a shed to sleep in if it rained. Every morning, the students woke up by the sun, went to sleep with the stars and moon above them, and slept on the soil of the Delaware region.

Crystal did not complain about the rigorous hiking program, but as a mother, I knew how tough it was for my spoiled baby. At home, she had her own bathroom and bedroom. Every meal was prepared by me. She only needed to put the food into her mouth herself. Now she needed to dig a hole for the bathroom and kill a bug on her arm by herself. Ouch! It was an incredible seven days of Outdoor Action.

When they returned to school, they'd already made good friends with each other. By the time the classes began in mid-September, they might not have too much foreign feelings about being in a big university like Princeton because they had met their hiking friends and become good buddies.

After freshman year, Crystal returned to the program to volunteer as a student "leader" for incoming "Frosh." That was what they called the newcomers. She enjoyed helping them until she graduated. It was a good start for new students. I was indeed impressed.

Going to college was the first time my daughter left my radar. I was unsure if she would be OK away from my full-time watch.

After her freshman class started, one Sunday morning, I was reading the local newspaper in the kitchen. As a new resident, I learned so much from reading books and newspapers. Mary had been my mentor and an excellent American cultural counselor, but she was not with me anymore. The October sun warmed my back and outlined the contour of my body on the wall. The coffee aroma filled the kitchen as I sipped.

Suddenly, an article caught my eye: a student from a neighboring town had committed suicide from depression. Looking at her picture, she was a beautiful teenager, a talented musician who played in Carnegie Hall. Her parents were immigrants from South Korea. Because of the privacy laws, they did not know their daughter was sick at the college. The school did not inform the family that she was on prescription drugs. It was too late when they found she had burned herself in the dorm. She died.

I was terrified by that news. What could I do to protect my child? There was a law preventing me from asking the school if my daughter was healthy or not, because she passed her eighteenth birthday.

I never was a believer in measuring maturity with a number. Kids learn to understand the world little by little. When they first left their childhood home and parents, there were many challenges in front of them. The age of eighteen was just a number. It did not mean anything to me.

I told myself that when it came to my child's safety, I did not care about the law. The law could get reversed later, if it did not work well. The harm to a child could never be undone.

I called Crystal's college academic advisor before her first midterm. The counselor was a young lady in Crystal's residential college. When I called her on a weekday afternoon, she quickly picked up my call in a charming tone.

The counselor assured me everything with my daughter was fine: "Crystal is a happy girl. She is doing well in her classes. I have a lot of students to worry about. She is not among them."

I felt at ease. I looked at the list of questions I had prepared to ask her. The next topic was varsity fencing. I had tried to talk Crystal into quitting sports because of the rigor of Princeton's academic standards. The fencing training took up a lot of her study time. She spent at least two hours daily on it, plus prep and shower time. On the weekends, they had to travel to other Ivy League schools for away games.

She refused. "Mom, I have to play and have fun. I can't always study." It was true.

Now she was an adult. I had lost my parental power of control. However, her college counselor assured me again that I shouldn't worry. Crystal was good under her supervision.

I hung up the phone, and my heart returned to where it was. With the good news, I could not wait to tell my daughter what the advisor said.

To my surprise again, Crystal was upset: "Mom, you checked up on me behind my back…?"

"It was good that your counselor said you were fine." I got offensive too: "I told you because I thought you'd be happy to hear it too. You know what? I still will call your school, but I'm not going to tell you because I paid for it."

I guess the "Paid for…" shut her up. She did not say anything at the other end of the telephone line.

I never called her advisor in the dorms again after that day. Children should let go, but little by little is the better way.

I remember that after being admitted to my college in China, every morning I sat in the classroom with ninety-five students. Looking at the newly painted white wall, there was no more Chairman Mao picture in 1978; instead, it was decorated with quotations from Confucius by a famous Chinese brush painting artist. It advised us to study hard and not waste time after the government had just wasted ten years of our valuable time. Every day in that classroom, I felt it was a privilege to be able to learn again. After the unavailability of a college education for so long, every other student felt the same way I did.

Now the educational environment Crystal had was way better than mine. The first time I visited her in school was during Parents Weekend. She was lying reading her books on the thick green lawn. It was in front of her gothic stone and slate dorm with old lead glass windows. The October sun shone on her, warm and lovely. The whole campus was peacefully colored by red leaves with grand castle-like buildings as a backdrop under the deep blue autumnal Jersey sky.

A film crew was busy shooting the movie *A Beautiful Mind* in the distance, but nobody cared about the famous big Hollywood stars here. I was amazed to see them as ordinary people for the first time.

All of this told me once more what "privilege" was. I felt the world was smiling at me again. What I could not get, my daughter was experiencing for me.

CHAPTER 25

A LIFE LEARNING

Unlike living in China, where families only deal with one race, one culture, and one political party, the diverse multicultural society in the U.S. made people want to know more about their racial and cultural background.

During Crystal's undergraduate years, she grew increasingly conscious of her heritage. As time passed by, she asked me ever more about Chinese culture and history. With the freedom to choose, she took some courses I would never imagine having the chance to take in China, like religion or film studies. When I was in college, we had no option to change majors. Once you decided on a major when you entered college, you must stick with it until graduation.

Crystal declared her major in college very late, saying she wanted to have a general liberal arts undergraduate education first, then she could decide what to do. I am jealous of the young people here who have so much freedom of choice for everything. From daily life to academic courses to political opinions, I did not have any of this luxury in my youth.

From the bottom of my heart, I hope they will realize and treasure the privilege that some young people in other parts of the world may not have. Once more, the diverse environment brought home to me the differences from my college years.

Similar to my fellow classmates, I did not have the freedom to choose courses I might be interested in. The college gave students class schedules that were designed for their majors. Schools controlled everything for students. You did what you were told to do. Innovative was unnecessary. If you wanted to be good, obedience was the only golden rule. I would not say I liked it, but I did it.

One day Crystal called me from Princeton with pride in her voice: "Mom, you know what? I have registered to take Chinese this semester."

She was a national Latin language gold medalist during her four years in high school. She had passed AP French AP Latin tests and both SAT II tests. Why on the earth did she want to get extra credits in a foreign language? I was lost.

I said to her in a puzzled voice, "Why? Didn't you have satisfied your foreign language requirements already?"

"Yes, I did, but I want to learn Chinese. It will be a handy tool in the business world."

Back in the school closure during Cultural Revolution, I taught math and Chinese to some kids in my *long-tang* for fun. My students and their mothers all liked the way I taught. That positive experience had given me the confidence to teach my daughter Chinese myself at home.

When she was about ten years old, I found there was a Chinese Sunday school nearby. I said to myself: if a Sunday school teacher could teach my daughter the language, I could to it too. Every weekend I sat down with Crystal using the new Chinese textbook my auntie sent from China. I explained the textbook story, then wrote the characters carefully for her to copy. Crystal copied the letters neatly, but in the next weekend's class, when I asked her the meanings of the words, she looked at me with loss in her eyes. She did not remember any of them. Language needs to be used. I had to give up after a month of trying.

Now she wanted to learn in school herself. It was a different initiative. I was wondering…

"I used to teach you Chinese at home, but you refused to learn," I reminded her.

"Yeah… but you didn't push me hard enough." She changed to being naughty.

It always was Mom's fault, no matter what. I never expected this time the result would be the opposite.

I got irritated, too. "Don't waste my tuition money. You do not need those credits. Take something more useful. You have enough Chinese built in."

"It's not about credits, Mom! It's that I want to learn more about my heritage. When the other Chinese mothers heard their kids wanted to take Chinese lessons, they were so happy and jumped to the air. You say I am wasting your money? I must take it." She hung up on me.

The Princeton version of the textbook impressed me when I got my first glimpse. The professors made it themselves with reasonable consideration for ABC, the American-born Chinese. Crystal was almost qualified for the name. She started in the second grade in a U.S. school, and English was now her first language.

Around 1955, the Chinese government issued a "Notice Regarding the Implementation of Simplified Chinese

Characters in All Schools." I learned simplified Chinese on the first day of elementary school. However, in Taiwan and Hong Kong, people still used the traditional characters and kept their own style of Pinyin letters for pronunciation. Two types of Chinese language systems existed simultaneously, especially in written Chinese.

The Princeton textbook cleverly showed the students both traditional and simplified Chinese characters. The left page was conventional Chinese with old Pinyin; the right page was simplified Chinese with Hanyu Pinyin, the new one that mainland China uses. This allowed the students to choose what they wanted to learn or do both, so they could meet their job requirements when they were in the workforce. The head of the Chinese department was not a Chinese native, but he and his team resolved the problem well.

When I read their textbook, I was extremely impressed. Most of the stories in the textbook were all about what might happen in an immigrant family daily. They were interesting and made the students want to read; I even enjoyed reading them with great curiosity. The textbook was made so interestingly down to the earth, it touched my heart.

Two months after the new semester started, the Thanksgiving holiday approached. Before the turkey dinner party, while preparing in the kitchen, I overheard Crystal talking to her cousin in the living room. They were laughing and reading her Chinese essay together.

I put the stuffing I was preparing on the counter and quickly looked into the living room. The essay was only a page long, neatly handwritten in a tiny font. There was a lot of content.

It was impossible! I knew how difficult the Eastern language was for a Western speaker. Crystal had never been sent to a Chinese school.

From that time, she mastered not only speaking Chinese but writing the language as well. The grammar and structure of the Chinese are very far from the English family. It was shocking for me. My eyes were wide open again.

"I don't know about the other subjects in Princeton, but if they have taught you the Chinese language to this level so quickly, I must say Princeton is a very good school." I said with satisfaction.

"It was not all about the school. I put effort into it too. I studied it hard every day." She wanted to get her credits too. Sure, she was responsible for it.

During Christmas vacation time, Crystal did another essay of two pages in tiny handwritten letters. I was even more amazed. If I forced her to learn, it wouldn't work. Her initiative was everything. As grateful as I was to the school, I had to give her credit.

Thinking back to my argument with Crystal at the beginning of the school year, I admitted that she had won. The language course was very well designed, but more importantly, I learned that she could do incredible things when she wanted to.

Back in China, graduation meant picking up that piece of paper called a *diploma*. Then I said goodbye to everyone I knew in school and went home. It was quite different here.

The ceremony started at the university chapel. It was solemn and elegant. When the organ prelude began, I felt a new sentiment touch me, from my ears to my heart, then to eyes.

Tears came down my cheeks. I asked myself what was happening, because I was not religious. It was an emotion filled with love. Perhaps it was because of the church music and the gorgeous chapel architecture; perhaps it was not anything in particular, just me. I was still unsure if God existed then, but at this point, I wished he lived and watched over me.

It was the end of May. The cicadas were humming untiringly. We sat under the shade of trees with the students in the next section, listening to the president's speech. Before she finished her talk, the president asked every graduate to stand up and turn around to say, "THANK YOU!" to all parents. Pride came to my heart more deeply than I could describe.

As a mother, I never complained or regretted my sacrifices from the day my baby was born. I never expected thanks that day. I was too preoccupied to think about how to handle things myself. Now, as the president said I was the reason for this happening, I felt the great honor of being a mother.

On this happy hot summer day, I naturally thought of another life-changing summer night, back in 1966. It took my education away from me and hundreds of thousands of kids in my generation in China. Today, my daughter earned it back by herself with hard work and an excellent learning environment in the United States. She could now call this land her new home. I am proud of her and thank God for it.

My grandmother was the first person who taught me "Never give up." Life could fail us. The Cultural Revolution happened without warning. But if we are strong and keep fighting, we can reach the other side. So be a fighter and be smart.

As my uncle and aunt taught me, money is essential to our lives, but life is not all about money. Be an independent thinker. Do not blindly obey, respect science, respect the truth, and always be honest with yourself. Never stop learning.

My two mothers showed me what love and sacrifice were. I shall always be kind to people and constantly be open-minded to learn new things. Be flexible and strong. That helped me greatly to adapt my new life in the new world.

My father was an excellent example of a hardworking man. He was an old-fashioned Chinese father who did not talk to his child openly heart-to-heart. I found it hard to understand him sometimes. But although Dad remained a mystery to me, he was always there for me when I needed support. He lived until he was 107 years old. Being constantly exercises and active with his friends as a consultant for the optical industry of Shanghai after he retired. Positive and optimistic attitude made him healthy and happy. He enjoyed good food and a glass of Chines wine every day. My father was the pillar of our family. He also brought laughers and held the family together during a tough time in the Cultural Revolution.

I owed them much more than what they gave to me. I love and miss them all.

AFTERWORD

After Princeton, Crystal worked at Citigroup and the World Bank, then attended INSEAD's MBA program in France. After that, she lived and worked in the United Kingdom for ten years before moving back to New York.

Jian Ping had moved back to Shanghai under a substitute program after ten years in Anhui. Under this policy, my biological father had to retire from his job so that his son could work at his company in Shanghai. Jian Ping worked there as an apprentice to a manager. He is still working as we speak. My biological parents passed away at the age of eighty-three and ninety-two years old.

China has been changed greatly since I left in 1987. I am happy to see the changes. A lot of political policies have been altered since I left China. The stories I have told in this book only reflect life before 1987.

While reading this memoir, I hope you will keep in mind that the Cultural Revolution was only a short but powerful stream in a long river of Chinese history: a period of time within thousands of years. But it was an incredibly important period. *We must never let it happen again.*

Talking to my nieces or nephews, sometimes I was surprised to learn that many of them did not know the Cultural Revolution well. Some of them had naïve questions, like 'Why did people not resist the Red Guards?' Some could not believe this ever happened. The descriptions of the Cultural Revolution in their school textbook were simple and minimal. This made me decide to write this memoir. As a Chinese person who lived through it, I am feeling the responsibility to pen it down and tell the world what happened in China in these days.

Looking back on my life path, I realized that I had travelled a long and bumpy road all the way. It was not easy, but it worth every step.